Without a Father

by Danny Crane

Danny Crane (signature)

Published by:
Empire Publishing, Inc.
3130 US Highway 220
Madison, NC 27025-8306
Phone: 336-427-5850 • Fax: 336-427-7372
www.empirepublishinginc.com

Library of Congress Control Number: 2012939260
ISBN Number: 978-0-944019-58-0

Published and printed in United States of America
1 2 3 4 45 6 7 8 9 10

Dedication

This book is dedicated to my lovely wife of fifty-three years, Maxine Weaver Crane. She wrote a booklet on "How to Write Your Story" and has given workshops in Virginia, North Carolina, and Florida. After attending these workshops, she inspired me, "a dumb old football coach," to write. One morning I awoke at three o'clock and began writing. When she got up, I told her that I had been writing. She asked to read what I had written. When she found out that it was my obituary, she said, "I am not going to put all of this in the newspaper...it would cost me a fortune!" I responded, "If we are going to sing one hundred of your favorite hymns at your funeral, surely you can put this obituary in the paper."

I thank Maxine for all of her encouragement, for her expertise in writing, for her many hours of typing and editing, and for her interest in my life story. If it had not been for my #1 earthly angel, Maxine, I would not have been motivated to write my story.

Chapter One

My First Earthly Angel, "Mom"

On a cold, windy, and snowy day, I was born November 5, 1932, in a farmhouse in LaGrange, Virginia, about ten miles east of the town of Culpeper, Virginia. My parents were Florence Elizabeth and Thomas Alfred Crane. The attending doctor was Dr. David Wright Kelly Jr. who was a local physician. During the Depression, doctors made house calls, even delivering babies. The farmhouse was owned by Florence's parents, Herbert and Nellie Brown.

At that time Florence did not know that my father would be murdered in Washington, D.C. There was no work available in Culpeper County so my dad found work in Washington D.C. and stayed in a rooming house Monday through Thursday. He came home on weekends. I was six months old when the murder occurred in the hall of the rooming house. After an investigation, it was determined that there were no clues and no leads. It has remained a mystery for over seven decades as to who murdered him. I have lived for seventy-nine years often wondering what kind of life I would have lived if my dad had not been murdered!

My father was buried in Lael Baptist Church Cemetery in Lignum, Virginia. He was nineteen years old when he died. Many people said that he was a very good-looking man with an exceptional personality. Mom told me that she loved him very much. After the funeral, we lived with Mom's parents.

Before her marriage, Mom attended Lignum High School and was a star basketball player. The school did not have a gym so the basketball team played outside. The season did not extend into winter because of the cold and snow during that time. Girls' basketball was played differently then. They played half-court basketball with each team having several teammates on each side of the court. The guards were on one side of the court and the forwards were on the other side. The players could not cross center court. Mom was about five-feet-ten inches and was very stout. She told me that players could only dribble the basketball twice. She was a very aggressive guard. No player ever ran over her. In fact, she would knock down a forward, either on purpose or accidentally, and then help them up. She refused to answer my questions when I asked her if she had ever been ejected from a game!

Mom was a hard worker and a very loving person. She worked as hard as any man. She worked at Safeway Foods for many years before she became ill with rheumatoid arthritis.

After four years of living with her parents and me in the farmhouse in LaGrange, she married Clyde Hiner. He was a very gentle, hard-working man employed by the State Highway Department, now known as VDOT. Mom and Clyde moved to Warrenton, Virginia, and left me with her parents, Herbert and Nellie Brown at LaGrange.

I have often wondered why I was left behind by my mother. I do remember on many occasions that we both cried almost every time she left. I begged to go home with her. She and Clyde visited almost every Sunday and I was very glad to see them.

Clyde was a good stepfather to me. He was a caring man and very kind. As years went by, Mom and Clyde had two girls, Peggy and Joan. They were pretty girls. I was proud to have two half-sisters, although I did not live with them.

Clyde was a foreman at the Virginia Highway Department for many years. When I was fourteen years old, Clyde got my uncle Estil and me a summer job at the Highway Department in Warrenton working nine-and-a-half hours a day making fifty-five cents an hour. All summer we cut bushes and dug post holes. Five days a week we stayed with Mom and her family. Every day I came home and said, "I cannot do this any longer. It is too hard for me." Every night Mom and Clyde encouraged Estil and me to go back to work the next day. Today, I am thankful we obeyed them. It is my philosophy that if Estil and I had quit, we would have been quitters in almost everything we did.

After Mom became ill with rheumatoid arthritis, she had many surgeries to correct joints which had become gnarled. At a young age, my half-sister Peggy had to do Mom's chores and take care of her younger sister, Joan. Eventually, Mom was so crippled that she had to enter a nursing home.

During my visits at her home, the hospital, or even the nursing home in Fredericksburg, Virginia, Mom never complained! The nurses and attendants said that she was an excellent patient. Before she died, she had suffered for ten years with rheumatoid arthritis. She went from two-hundred pounds to seventy pounds.

Mom died at the age of forty-nine in 1964. She left me with encouragement and motivation for life. I carry her attitude that "no matter what hardship you have in life, the good Lord will see you through it." She also taught me that "whatever you do, do it to the best of your ability."

Chapter Two

My Second Earthly Angel, "Daddy"

My grandparents Nellie and Herbert Brown had seven children: Roy Hamilton, Hazel Virginia, Florence Elizabeth, Katherine Kelly, Maxine Odell, Stanley Eugene, and Estil Herbert. I became the eighth child in that farmhouse. After awhile, I began calling my grandmother "Mama" and my grandfather "Daddy."

Our farmhouse consisted of six rooms and a path (to the outhouse). It had two screened-in porches and one front porch without a screen. Since we had no electricity, we had to use a hand pump for pumping water out of our well, which was located just outside the screened-in porch on the west side of the house. We had no indoor bathroom; therefore, we had no bathtub. Every time it rained, we collected rain water in tubs to be used for baths and washing clothes. During the summer when we experienced extremely dry spells, the well went dry. When that happened, Daddy took Stanley, Estil and me to Carrico Mills (about two miles away) to take a bath in a small river called Mountain Run. We took Ivory soap because it floats, a wash cloth, and a towel. Keeping the soap from floating down the river was a task. Recently Joyce Waugh and Patsy Margart were visiting Margie and Estil Brown at LaGrange. The "Ivory soap" story came up. Patsy laughed and said, "We walked through cow poop to get to the river to take our baths and after we bathed, we walked back through the cow poop to go back to the house!" When we finally got electricity, we built an indoor bathroom and lived the "life of Riley."

The small farm at LaGrange was a busy place. During the Depression, life was hard for most people, but our farm was self-sufficient. We had chickens (hens and roosters), hogs, cows, turkeys, a horse, a mule, guineas, cats, and a dog. We raised hay, wheat, corn, and had a huge garden. We had apple, cherry, pear, and damson trees. We also had a grape arbor. Almost everything we needed was available on the farm. We bought staples at the store such as coffee, tea, sugar, salt, pepper, and canning supplies.

We killed chickens, turkeys, and hogs to eat. Killing a chicken was not too bad. One person held the chicken by the feet and another person cut off its head with a sharp butcher knife. It was disturbing to watch the chicken flop around until it died. When our visiting cousins Joyce and Patsy were around, they couldn't stand the sight of the blood all over the ground. They disappeared quickly. To hypnotize a chicken, we put the chicken's head under one wing, rocked it back and forth, and it would lie there until we took the head from under the wing. After we chopped the head off, we dipped the chicken in hot water and picked the feathers off. Finally, we "field dressed" it. We cleaned out the internal organs and took the chicken to Mama to cut up and fry.

Hog killing was quite a complicated event. Each year Daddy raised four hogs to be used for meat. We had Negro neighbors, Uncle Ben and Nathan, who went to farms before Christmas to slaughter hogs. The three of us boys always helped whether we wanted to or not. Three of my jobs were to hold the hind legs of the hog while it was being slaughtered, to scrape the hair off the hog with a zinc canning top, and after the hog was dropped into hot water, I had to pull off the toenails with a large hook. If the butcher did not stick the knife in far enough, the hog would get up and stagger until it fell and died. Some farmers used a twenty-two caliber rifle to shoot the hog between the eyes before being slaughtered, but Daddy did not believe in that. One time as I was pulling the toenails off a hog, the big hook slipped and the sharp part went into the thumb pad of my hand. The pain was severe. My hand was bleeding profusely. Daddy got a clean rag, poured turpentine on it, and said, "It will get well before you get married!" That was the last thing I wanted to hear! After a short rest, he said, "Daniel, it is time to get back to work." With extreme pain, I went back to scraping hair off the hogs, but I did not pull off anymore toenails. One of the helpers took over that job. After several weeks of healing, a huge scar remained on my hand and still does. From that day forward, I always hated "hog killing time," but the fresh cooked pork sure tasted good!

Daddy had a shop and was a master at many trades. He even had a mill where he ground wheat into flour and corn into meal. It was interesting to see him after grinding. He looked like a ghost, or a snowman.

As a blacksmith, he made horseshoes, welded metals, repaired wells, shod horses, made wagon wheels, kept beehives, killed hogs, gardened, and even was the postmaster at LaGrange for years. Daddy made all of the girls in the family rings made out of horseshoe nails. Joyce Crane Waugh and Patsy Brown Morgart still treasure theirs today.

When the post office closed, a sign with the name of LaGrange was moved from the main highway.

Daddy was a tall, muscular man who was very strong despite having polio. He had to stay in the bed for a year as he recovered from polio. During that time, his brother John A. Brown owned a grocery store in Lignum and delivered all groceries to Daddy's home. John kept a ledger at his store with a list of all groceries that were purchased that year. The total for the year was one-hundred-fifty-three-dollars and twenty seven cents. His daughter Thelma helped him to run the store. Later, when her father died, she became the sole owner of the store. Also, as time passed, she gave up the store and became a mail carrier for the Lignum Post Office. On Sundays, she played the piano at Lael Baptist Church. Many years later, she was murdered and the trial was quite confusing. I'm not sure if the killer was ever punished.

That disease left Daddy with a severe limp in one leg, but he did not let that handicap slow him down.

In fact he taught us to swim when we were quite young. He took us to the Rapidan River at Germanna and said, "This is how you do it." He showed us how to "dog paddle." We copied what he did, and soon we were swimming.

On our farm Daddy had a mule to help with the farm work. It was very tame and obedient. One day after all work was done, I decided to ride the mule. After putting on the bridle, I got on the mule bareback since we didn't own a saddle. I directed the mule onto the gravel road in front of the house. After getting out of sight of the house, I wanted to see how fast that mule could run. While we were going in a full gallop, the mule stumbled and I went forward over its head into the gravel. I was stunned and afraid of what Mama and Daddy would do to me. I did not break anything but really got scraped from the fall. I was bleeding on my hands and knees. The mule was okay. I led the mule back to the barn and went to see Mama and Daddy. I "fessed up" to what I had done. If I had not been bleeding so much, I believe that I would have gotten the worst switching I have ever had. They did give me a severe scolding and I promised, "I will never do that again!"

Mama and Daddy were members at Hopewell Methodist Church in Lignum, Virginia. Daddy was one of the main leaders of that church. Many times he was "called on" to pray either in Sunday School or during the worship service. He is the one who taught me to pray. When he prayed, he would always kneel down.

Each Sunday morning we were told to "get up and get ready for church." We did not have to ask, "Are we going to church today?" We knew we would be there unless we were ill or if snow was too deep to get there. Daddy did not accept the excuse, "Church is boring."

During the winter months, Daddy, Estil, Stanley, and I went to church early to start the fire in the wood stove so it would be warm when the congregation arrived. The church at that time was one large room. Also, we cut wood and hauled it to the church for the fires.

All three of us boys slept in one upstairs bedroom with no central heat. There was a grate in the floor directly above the old wood stove that was downstairs. On cold mornings, we would shove each other around to see who would get to stand over the heat. I always ended up last because I was the youngest.

In the summer, Daddy and the three boys mowed the cemetery beside the church, which was about one acre. During this time, there were no engine-powered mowers. We pushed the mower with every muscle in our bodies. There were no power-driven weed eaters, so we cut grass around the tombstones with a sickle.

Several years later, power-driven lawnmowers were made. Daddy bought one for our home so we also used it at the church cemetery. The first day we had it, Estil and I were mowing grass at the farm when a Negro gentleman brought a wagon wheel to Daddy's shop to be repaired. He had a young son about our age who had never seen a power-driven lawn mower. He came to where Estil and I were. He wanted to try it out. I was holding the handle and he tried to grab it. As I looked at him, he drew a knife on me. I grabbed for it and he

13

cut my hand, which still has a scar today. Estil became so angry that he grabbed the knife, threw it aside, and started beating the boy. Daddy heard the screaming and came and pulled Estil off the boy. I believe that Estil would have killed him if Daddy had not stopped the fight. From that moment on, Estil and I became "blood brothers."

The boys' Sunday School class was taught by Frances Brown. We three boys were very active, to say the least. We were not bad boys, but we were "live wires." I think back to those days and I am glad that I wasn't our teacher. Frances Brown did a wonderful job teaching us about Jesus. In fact, she was one of the main people who encouraged me to accept the Lord and join the church.

Our home did not have electricity since there were no power lines in that area. Many nights, homework was done by using oil lamps which were very dim. We had one mantle lamp which was brighter than oil lamps but the light did not cover a large area. From a May 2, 1941, ledger of Daddy's, there is a complete list of the costs he had to pay to install electricity by City Electrical Company in Charlottesville, Virginia:

Contract for wiring house	$75.00
2 safety plugs	2.50
1 Bath Room Lite	1.50
1 Bed Room Lite	1.00
Dining Room Lite	3.00
Living Room Lite	3.00
1 switch Back Porch	6.50

Heat was provided by wood stoves. Stanley (who was two years older than I) and Estil (who was eleven months older than I) were taught to do hard work at an early age. We helped with the garden, milked cows, slopped the hogs, made hay using pitch forks, thrashed wheat, cut corn (put it in shocks, shucked it, put it into the corn house, removed the corn from the ear with a corn sheller and prepared it for milling), killed chickens and hogs to eat, and helped with sawing wood with a crosscut saw.

Cutting and splitting wood was a very hard task. Daddy would "wear out" the three of us sawing wood. He pulled on one end of the crosscut saw and we pulled on the other end. We did not last long at a time, so we alternated pulling the saw. Daddy not only pulled on his end, but probably pushed on his end to help us!

Daddy also had a large saw that was run by an engine to saw slabs of wood bought from a sawmill at Lignum. It was a very dangerous task so he constantly reminded us of what to do so that we would not get hurt. One of the boys held one end of the wood and Daddy held the other as it was fed into the saw. Only slabs of wood were sawed this way.

The logs that were cut in the woods with the crosscut saw were cut into pieces in the woods and were taken to the house and put in a pile to be split with an ordinary axe, not a six pound splitting mall like we have today. Sometimes a wedge had to be used to split larger pieces of wood. One had to be extremely strong and accurate to split wood properly. One day Daddy told us a story about an uncle of his who went out to split wood too early after a thunderstorm. As he held the axe over his head, lightning struck the metal part of the axe. The metal melted and ran down his body and killed him. Daddy always reminded us to never go outside too early after a thunderstorm ends.

In the late 1960's. at Deale Mountain Farm which was owned by Maxine's dad, the girls and I were seated on the front porch in a rocking chair. A thunderstorm came up quickly. I decided it was the perfect time to teach my young girls Cheryl and Cathie how to not be afraid of lightning. I told them, "Light travels one mile in five seconds and if we count the number of seconds (one-thousand-and-one for each second) between seeing the lightning and hearing the thunder, we can determine approximately how far away the storm is. If we count ten seconds, the storm will be approximately two miles away; therefore, we should be safe from being struck by lightning." We had been doing that for several minutes and determined the storm was two miles away. All of a sudden, the sound of thunder occurred at the same time as the lightning! The girls and I ran inside as fast as we could to join their mother who was cowering inside the house. Maxine's mother had always made her afraid of storms. I guess I was a poor example for a parent-teacher. Today, people are taught that if one can hear thunder, lightning is close enough to strike a person.

Each spring Mama strongly encouraged Nathan Hansborough to burn off the broom sage field so trees would not grow and hide her view of the country. Daddy and the three boys always helped him to do that.

At Christmas, Daddy opened his roll-top desk

and put out a small amount of candy and nuts. When that was eaten, he did not put out anymore until the next night. My favorite candy was chocolate covered peanuts and they still are today.

Santa Claus always came to see us. During the end of the Great Depression, times were very difficult. The three of us were lucky to get some candy, nuts, raisins, an orange, a toy, and a shirt and trousers. If I got a new piece of clothing, I was very excited since most of my clothes were handed down from Stanley and Estil. Occasionally, I would get a ball, bat, or catcher's mitt. Regardless of what we got or didn't get, we were always reminded of what Christmas meant - celebrating the virgin birth of our Lord and Savior Jesus Christ.

One Christmas when I was five years old, Stanley, Estil, and I ran down the steps to see what Santa had brought us. Each of us had a complete matching cowboy suit with a holster and two cap pistols for each side! We felt like we were real cowboys when we put those on. I wanted to wear mine to church but Mama would not allow that. The main reason that we got so excited with the suits and pistols was that on Saturday afternoons, we were taken to the Ritz Theater in Culpeper to see Gene Autry, Roy Rogers, Hop-along Cassidy, and other cowboy movies. It cost us twenty-five cents to go to a movie, but we could not afford to buy popcorn or candy. Naturally, we had to play out the movie when we got home. We always appreciated whatever we got no matter how small it was.

I got a baseball mitt one year. I was so proud of it that I slept with it for quite a while. The value system that was preached to us was everlasting. I still appreciate the little things in life. Thank God that I am not a hoarder.

During that particular time, fireworks were used, probably more than on the fourth of July. We had Roman candles, cherry bombs, rockets, torpedoes, sparklers, and others. We had to be careful with the Roman candles because occasionally one would backfire. I was holding one in my hand one time and it backfired...only burning my hand enough to cause it to blister. The good Lord was looking after me as He has always done.

One day, Daddy took Stanley, Estil, and me to Culpeper to see our dentist Doctor Palmer. Prior to that, Daddy always pulled our teeth when necessary. He had a pair of dental forceps. I only let him pull one baby tooth of mine since it hurt so much. I always pulled my own, working it back and forth until it came out. At the dentist office neither one of us wanted to go first so Daddy made the oldest, Stanley, go first. After Stanley was seated in the chair, Estil and I heard a yell. We ran out of the dentist's office and down the main street of Culpeper. Daddy, crippled in one leg, came yelling to find us. When we heard him, we came to him knowing that we had to face the unknown and would have to face the dentist. As well as I can remember, it really wasn't too bad.

Daddy taught me to be thankful for all that we had and also taught me how to work and do my best. He was not the type of man to tell us that he loved us, but I always knew that he loved me. He never switched us but corrected by talking to us. He left the switching to

Mama.

In the 1930's, Daddy's brother Luther had a country store about two-hundred yards from our house. We had no radio, so we would go to his store to listen to the fights of Joe Louis, Max Schmeling, and Billy Conn. Many people came to hear those fights and to tell stories by the "potbellied" wood stove or on the front porch. One of the treats for Stanley, Estil, and I was to get a pepsi or coke and pour a bag of salty peanuts in it. We would drink and chew the nuts as we drank. Also, we could buy a bag of candy for one penny.

After Luther died and the store was closed permanently, we shopped in Lignum with Daddy's brother, John, and his daughter Thelma. There was another store in Lignum owned by Harry and Ab Willis, which gave "Uncle John" competition. The Willis' store was directly across from the Lignum School which was both elementary and high school at that time. Students were told not to go across the highway to that store at any time. Administrators and teachers were very strict so we had to obey. We knew that if we got into trouble at school, we would be in more trouble when we got home!

Daddy was well known for paying any debts that he had. When Mama was in the hospital, he sold his best cow to pay the hospital bill which was $702.57. When she died May 22, 1959, he paid the funeral bill of $844.57.

In January of 1960, Daddy signed his last will and testament. He tried to be fair to all of his children. The last statement in the will was: "SIXTH: I direct all of my net estate, on being liquidated, shall be equally divided among my children with, however, my grandson, Daniel Crane, taking a child's part. In other words, I wish my net estate to be divided equally among the following residuary legatees: Roy H. Brown, Hazel Brown Crane, Catherine B. Jones, Florence B. Hiner, Maxine B. Crane, Stanley Brown, Estil Brown, and Daniel Crane." Maxine and I bought a kitchen table and chairs for our first home with the money that I received.

Daddy was born January 6, 1888. He died November 9, 1961. During his later years, he had a problem with high blood pressure. Many times after Mama died, we saw him shed tears as he missed his wonderful wife. I never heard them say a harsh word to each other at any time. He was the strongest Christian that I have ever known. I was proud to be called "son."

Chapter Three

My Third Earthly Angel, "Mama"

Grandmother Brown, "Mama," was a lady who weighed over two hundred pounds and she had a heart just as large. She was a strict disciplinarian and when she spoke, we had better listen or pay the consequences. She believed in the Bible and practiced what it taught such as "train up a child in the way he should go, and when he is old he will not depart from it." Also, she reared her children to "be seen and not heard."

Mama taught Stanley, Estil, and me proper manners such as saying "thank you…please…yes sir…no sir…no ma'am…" Today as I hear young people respond with good manners, I thank them for good manners and tell them to thank those who taught them.

Mama was a good Mother, a good Grandmother, a good cook, a good seamstress, a good laundress, a good housekeeper, a good Christian, and a good wife. She was the captain of our household. Anytime one of us needed a switching, she was the one to do it. In fact, she made us go to the tree and pull our own switch. She switched us but not to the point of being abusive. We had a dog, Dopey, that always tried to protect us. Mama had to switch Dopey so he would run and hide, allowing her to switch us.

On Sundays, Mama did not always go to Sunday School and church with us because she had to cook dinner for the entire family which was usually more than thirty people. Whenever we had church at night or during revival, she attended unless she was preparing a fried chicken dinner for the preacher in charge of the revival. The preacher at Hopewell Methodist Church in Lignum had a circuit of many churches such as Richardsville, Brandy, and other places. Hopewell Methodist Church had preaching two times a month.

One Christmas Frances Brown encouraged Stanley, Estil, and me to sing at the Christmas services. "We Three Kings" was selected for us to sing. I don't think that we ever practiced. Many times at church we did not have a piano player. I do not have a very good singing voice. Estil is a little worse than I. Stanley, well I won't mention that. We sang (?) at the service, and boy, was I glad when we finished. I'm sure the congregation was glad, also.

Several years later, I was asked to sing a solo. The congregation forgot how poor I was at singing and asked me to sing "Away in a Manger." At this time we still did not have a piano player. I had to sing a cappella. Once again the congregation was happy when I got through. That ended my singing in public.

On Sundays we played baseball, rode the horse or mule, played tag, and played football. I remember the adults sitting around talking while the boys thought of things to do. Hazel and Joe Crane, my aunt and uncle, had five boys: Herbert Clayton, Harvey Joe, Allen Thomas, Roy Samuel, and Jerry Wayne. Two of them, Clayton and Harvey, were about the age of Stanley, Estil, and me. We really enjoyed playing together. One Sunday, someone in our group came up with the idea of playing the "mystery pocketbook game."

Route 3 was a highway within one-half of a mile from our house. There was a culvert under the road that was tall enough for us to hide in it. One day we tied a strong string on a woman's pocketbook and placed it in the middle of the road. We took the other end with us and hid in the culvert. It didn't take long before we heard a car slow down. The driver saw the pocketbook! He slammed on his brakes and backed up to where he had seen the pocketbook. In the meantime, we pulled the pocketbook into the culvert. Several drivers became very angry and confused. We had a hard time disguising our laughter. We never let Mama know about our trickery.

An old rock quarry was not far from our house. The five boys (Stanley, Estil, Clayton, Harvey, and I) went there to swim. Many times our parents did not know where we were. They were too busy telling stories or talking politics on a hot Sunday afternoon. Our favorite thing to do at the quarry was to dive out of a tall tree into the water and see if we could dive down and touch the bottom. Not all of us dove from the tree as it was about ten feet above the water. Each of us tried to go under water to touch the bottom. None of us was successful in doing so. Our heavenly angel was looking after us while we were doing those things. Many years later, we found out that the old quarry had junk cars and other construction materials at the bottom. If we had encountered any of those things, it would have been impossible for us to survive. Of course, we did not tell Mama about going to the rock quarry until many years later.

One day Mama sent Estil and me to the garden to pick green beans. It was a Saturday, the day before the Brown clan was coming to Sunday dinner. She gave us a five-gallon bucket to fill. We packed half of the bucket with tomatoes and filled the rest of the bucket with green beans. We took the bucket to the house and went to play. We had not been playing long before we heard a loud familiar voice, "Estil and Daniel, come here right now!" She had discovered what we had done. We had to go back to the garden to pick an entire five-gallon bucket of beans.

When it was time for Estil to enroll in school, he would not go to school unless I went. Mama called the superintendent of Culpeper County Schools, Paul Hounshell. She explained the situation to him and he told her, "Daniel cannot attend because he is too young." At that time, school systems did not have kindergarten, so at six years old, one went to the first grade. Mama did not stop trying to get permission for me to go to school with Estil although I was not six years old.

After several calls to Mr. Hounshell and the School Board, it was approved for me to go to school with Estil. Mr. Hounshell told Mama, "Daniel will be allowed to go to school but he will have to behave and do all the work and not get any credit." That meant that I could go to school with Estil, but I would have to be in the first grade at Lignum School again the next year.

Mama told Mr. Hounshell, "I have raised seven children who know how to behave, and I am raising Daniel the same way." She also added, "If he gets into trouble at school, he will be punished at home as well." As well as I can remember, I never got into trouble at school in elementary, high school, undergraduate school, and graduate school!

Estil wanted to be in the same grade as I. He planned to fail the first grade so we could be classmates... a clever decision for a six-year-old! It happened. He failed the first grade and we were classmates again.

Both of us were promoted to the second grade. The class work was harder and apparently Estil's poor work habits in the first grade were carried over into the second grade. He failed the second grade and I passed to the third grade. We were no longer classmates, but were very close. He was my uncle but he was more like a brother.

Elementary school work seemed very easy for me. Maybe because I would do my homework by a kerosene lamp every night. If we had a book, I would always read ahead.

During recess, we played tag, cowboys and Indians, baseball, softball, football, or some other sport. We had a horizontal bar for pull-ups. Not only did I do pull-ups but I did what I call "skin the cat." To perform this feat, I took hold of the bar, lifted my legs over the bar, and lifted the rest of my body over the bar back to the hanging position. Perhaps, that helped me to become a good pole-vaulter. One time during recess, my teacher Mrs. Carolyn Colvin had a supervisor to visit us on the playground. She asked me to do pull-ups for our visitor. I did twenty-five that day which not only impressed my teacher but also her supervisor.

One thing that I failed to mention about recess was that the boys wrestled each other when Mrs. Colvin was not watching. One day while wrestling, my opponent put his leg behind mine and threw me down. Before the fall, I heard a bone snap. I was taken to the doctor in Culpeper to have the large bone in my lower leg, the tibia, set and have a cast put on it. When Mama asked the teacher how it happened she said, "He was playing outside and when he turned around his leg snapped." I was kept in bed several days until I could get up and walk on crutches. I was on crutches for six weeks. I really missed my activities of running and playing.

One week after having the cast removed from my leg, we had a snowstorm of about twelve inches. Stella Payne, one of our neighbors, had planned to board the Trailways bus at Lignum. The dirt and gravel road in front of our house had not been scraped. Only one lane on Route 3 from Sherwood Farm to Lignum had been cleared, which was about one mile. Stella had to meet the bus that day, so she called Mama to explain her predicament. It was impossible to drive any vehicle, even with chains on the tires, to get to Route 3. Stella asked Mama if the two of us boys would take her to Lignum on a sled. I always enjoyed the snow, especially sledding on the hills. The only problem was that my healing broken leg was still weak.

Mama told Estil and I to take Stella to Lignum. We were very excited to go out, not only to help Stella but also to enjoy the sledding. We put Stella and her suitcase on the large sled and headed to Lignum. We alternated pulling the sled. When we got to a long hill, Estil and I both pulled. My leg did not bother me too much until we were on the way home. That exercise must have been good physical therapy because soon after that, my leg healed.

Estil and I were great buddies at a young age and still are today. I consider him one of my closest friends. One Sunday afternoon while Mama and Daddy were entertaining family, Estil and I decided to collect some cigarette butts to smoke on Monday after school. Little did we know that Mama saw what we were doing.

After school on Monday, we took the cigarette butts and went to the wood stove in the kitchen to get some matches. Once again, Mama saw what we were doing.

We went behind the shop and lit up. We hadn't puffed much when we heard a familiar voice, "Estil and Daniel, come here right now!" Perhaps she saw smoke! We hurriedly scrambled around and extinguished the evidence of cigarettes.

When we got to the house, she said, "You boys have been smoking."

We replied, "No, ma'am." She smelled our breaths which made us guilty.

Once again, Mama made us choose our own switch. Also, she had to switch our dog "Dopey" so he would be afraid to protect us. After the switching, we had to stick out our tongues and she put pepper on them and said, "Go to your room and smoke at both ends for awhile."

When supper time arrived, we were not called to eat, and we were really smoking at both ends. About an hour or so later, Daddy called us to come downstairs and eat. We asked, "Are you sure we can?" I believe if it hadn't been for him, we might not have had supper that night.

I did not smoke anymore until I was twenty-two years old, while I was in the United States Army.

I found it was easy to stop smoking, I stopped several times a day for a year! Eventually I gave up smoking in 1967 with a lot of difficulty since I was smoking three packs a day. To my knowledge, I think Estil never started smoking. I am very thankful that Mama raised me to do right and not spare the rod. Once again she used a quote from the Bible, "If you spare the rod, you will spoil the child." Perhaps more parents today should think about that and take some action.

Mama taught me discipline and hard work. She taught me how to do housework like washing and waxing floors. I did not mind that, but I hated dusting furniture!

Mama was born January 30,1892. She died March 22, 1959. She developed asthma during the late 1940's. As time passed, she developed a serious asthmatic reaction. In fact, it became so bad that I had to learn to give her shots. The first time I gave her a shot, the needle would not go in. I almost fainted! She told me, "You have to push it in real hard. It won't hurt me." From then on, I had no problem giving her shots for asthma. At times her breathing was loud and fast. I thought that she was going to die. Mama was a wonderful Christian, a great cook, a stern disciplinarian, and a very loving and caring person.

She carried out the perfect role as Mother, although she was my grandmother.

Chapter Four

My Fourth Earthly Angel, Albert Thomas Howard, Jr..

On December 7, 1941, the Japanese bombed Pearl Harbor and President Franklin D. Roosevelt declared war on Germany and Japan. This was the beginning of World War II. I was in the fourth grade. I did not understand the consequences of war, but I knew it was a scary time. My older Uncles were either volunteering for the military service or were being drafted. Many commodities such as gasoline, sugar, and meats were rationed because of the war.

Daddy joined the Civil Air Patrol in the Lignum-LaGrange area. Many nights Stanley, Estil, and I went with Daddy and spent the night at Lignum Elementary School (only when we did not have to go to school the next day). We logged all airplane flights including time, flight path, etc. The information was phoned immediately to the Civil Air Patrol. Also, we had practice air raids as we had to make sure all windows in all houses were totally dark. Even kerosene lamps had to be extinguished.

In 1946, while I was in the seventh grade, I had my first girlfriend, Thelma Ryder. Her youth group at Lael Baptist Church had planned a hayride for Friday night. She invited me to go but Mama told me I could not go. At ten o'clock that night, I got a phone call stating, "Thelma fell off the truck and one of the rear wheels ran over her and killed her." I had never had to deal with death before. The only sadness that I had known was being raised without my father and being left behind by my birth mother.

I was sad for a long time. I was too young to understand "puppy love." I had never kissed her. She had been so kind and understanding to me. She was someone who listened as I talked. When I went to the funeral home on family night, I was crying and did not know what to do. I went to the casket and kissed her on the cheek. It was another real tragedy in my life. I often wondered if she would have fallen off the truck if I had gone or would I have fallen off too. Only God knows.

Being in the seventh grade at this time, I was looking forward to entering Culpeper County High School the next year. It didn't happen. The state of Virginia passed a law that an eighth grade would be added before a student could become a freshman. The law required twelve grades for graduation rather than eleven years. I was very disappointed.

As a young boy, I had curly hair which was not cut very often. In the eighth grade, I was taken to town to get a haircut. I did not like combing all of that hair each day, so I told the barber, Mr. Sophia, to give me a G.I. haircut. He almost shaved my head. Mama did not like it. She made me wear a cap until it grew out.

On Sunday afternoons, Aunt Katherine's husband, Jack Jones, brought his guitar to the farm and played for us. I became very interested in "hillbilly" music. He told me to listen to the Grand Ole Opry from Nashville, Tennessee, on Saturday nights on Station WSM. I asked Jack if he would teach me to play the guitar. He agreed. He began by teaching me chords on his guitar. That Christmas, Santa Claus brought me a Montgomery Wards guitar, the best gift I got that year.

Jack told me to practice G, C, and D chords until I could make the correct sounds. Stanley did not like "hillbilly" music so I could not practice inside the farmhouse. Since we still had no electricity, we had a "johnny house" for our bathroom. It was a four-seater…a "Daddy" sized hole, a "Mama" sized hole, and two different sizes for children. When it was vacant, that is where I practiced with my guitar.

The next step was for Jack to play with me and instruct me as to when to change chords. I became so interested that I wanted to go to the Ryman Theater in Nashville, Tennessee, to perform. More on that later!

At Culpeper County High School in 1946, I met Coach A.T. Howard who was my eighth grade English teacher. I had no idea that one day he would legally adopt me.

In the 40's education required a lot of rote memory. One day Coach Howard required all class members to recite by memory the poem "Thanatopsis" by William Cullen Bryant. We were supposed to stand before the whole class and repeat it. When my turn came, he called on me and said, "Danny Crane, you are next."

I told him, "I can't do it."

"Did you learn it?" he asked.

I said, "Yes, sir, but I can't do it."

He said, "I want to see you after class." I met with him after class and he was very nice. He encouraged me to recite it the next day. He also said, "If you do not recite it tomorrow, I will call your grandmother." You'd better believe that I recited it the next day!

In the meantime, Coach Howard became the assistant coach in football. Ed Null was head coach. Coach Howard heard from the physical education teacher that Stanley, Estil, and I had athletic ability. He asked us to come out for football. We told him, "Mama won't let us play. She is afraid that we will get hurt." We also knew that we were needed to help on our small farm.

The next year when Coach Howard became the head football coach and Coach Null became his assistant, he visited Mama to encourage her to let us play football. Coach Howard was a U.S. Marine in WWII and Mama was tough as a Marine, also. The three of us boys felt like we would not be able to play. Coach Howard said to Mama, "These boys have athletic ability and I would like to have them on my team."

Mama said, "Mr. Howard, I hear that you use some bad language on the football field."

"Yes, ma'am. I learned that language as a Marine in the war."

She said, "If you do not use bad language, I will

let them play football for you." Stanley, Estil, and I were so elated, we didn't know what to do. In fact, Mama liked the coach so much that she invited him to stay for dinner. And he did.

At this time REA had installed electric lines in our area and we had electricity for the first time. We helped Daddy put in an indoor bathroom (the total cost was $73.33) and helped him to install a septic system. For the first time in our lives we used the indoor bathroom and did not freeze at the "johnny house."

Stanley, Estil, and I worked in the summer to earn money for clothes, movies, etc. Television was available in our area if we put an antenna on the roof. Daddy could not afford a television set, so the three of us bought one. We only received four channels from Washington, D.C. which was about sixty-five miles away. Although the reception was not very clear, Daddy enjoyed it more than we did. He stayed up long after we went to bed to watch his favorite show, professional wrestling. Sometimes he yelled so loud that we would awaken us. We would chuckle, turn over, and go back to sleep.

Coach Howard played high school football at Culpeper High School, at Bluefield College for two years, and at Hampton Sydney for three years. When he came out of the marines, he coached the Marine football team at Quantico, Virginia, and Hampton Sydney before coming to Culpeper.

During the summer of 1946, one year after WWII ended, a revival was taking place. Pete Turner, the young preacher, was staying with us. I accepted Jesus as my

Savior and was baptized at Hopewell Methodist Church in Lignum. Pete was in training to be a minister, and he was very instrumental in getting the three of us boys to accept Christ. That summer, he met one of my cousins, Lois Seay, and a few years later married her.

In 1947 Stanley and I "tried out" for the football team at CCHS. Estil had to wait an additional year before he could go out because he was in the eighth grade. At that time, an athlete only had four years to play on a team. Mama gave us permission to play if we could do farm chores when we got home from practice. The major problem was that we had no transportation for the ten miles from practice to our home. Coach Howard took care of that problem. He enlisted several business men...Pete Davies, Pete Norris, Rawley Coleman, Jack Davies, and others to take us home after practice. Sometimes Coach Howard took us.

The first day of practice we were equipped with shoulder pads, thigh pads, knee pads, a pair of football cleats, a jersey, a "leather" football helmet (not the kind that folded up and fit in the hip pocket). It was the kind as seen in the movie *Leather Heads*. We had no mouthpiece nor face masks. They came later.

After getting dressed, we had to walk to a practice field. Every afternoon we walked from the high school on West Street, over Mountain Run bridge, to the Old Rixeyville Road field. The walk was about a half- mile from our school. Since we had no other shoes to wear on the hard surfaced road, we wore out a pair of football cleats every two weeks. The walk to the field was easy, but the walk back was very tiring. Coach

Howard practiced us very hard because he wanted us to be winners. He was a real motivator so we had good football teams at CCHS.

Stanley and I ran and tried to get conditioned several weeks before practice started since we heard that Coach Howard was an ex-marine and was very tough. Stanley made the varsity team as a starting right guard and defensive nose guard. He was one of the toughest players I have ever seen. Before a game he would get so excited that he would throw up, but he would be fine at kick-off time.

Stanley did not have to attend the eighth grade so he graduated two years ahead of me. Coach Howard got him a football scholarship to the University of Richmond but things did not work out for him there. The next year, he got a football scholarship to Emory and Henry in southwestern Virginia and was one of the main blockers for their All-American running back, Bob Miller. They played for Coach Conley Snidow there. Stanley was so rough at football practice that his coach told him not to be so rough when he blocked and tackled his own team players. Coach Snidow was afraid one of his players might get hurt, especially Bob Miller.

When it was finally time for my first high school football game, I was on the junior varsity team. I learned skills from Coach Ed Null, our backfield coach. The Good Lord gave me the talent of quickness and speed. The first junior varsity game was at home with James Monroe from Fredericksburg. I was the starting wingback and safety. I scored three touchdowns in that game. We won the game. Coach Howard moved me to the varsity team for the next game.

The offense that we ran was the single wing with an unbalanced line. The position that I played was wingback. I was promoted to second string varsity behind William Jenkins. He was very fast. In elementary school, there was no one who could run faster than I, but in high school William could outrun me. He taught me how to run faster simply by watching him and being motivated by him. Our team had an 8-1-1 record that year. I played in many games that year because our first team scored so many points that the subs had a chance to play in many games.

In the spring of my freshman year, Coach Howard encouraged me to go out for track. He wanted his running backs to improve their running skills especially by running the high hurdles (a practice that would cause a runner to pick up his knees higher as he ran). He not only wanted me to run the 100-yard-dash and the 220-yard-dash, but he also wanted me to learn how to high jump, pole vault, broad jump, and even learn how to throw the twelve-pound shot and the three-pound discus. He told me that he didn't know all of the techniques, but he would take me to the private school Woodberry Forest in Madison County, Virginia, to learn them.

After football season, Coach Howard took me to Woodberry Forest. We met with Coach Leonard Dick who had many years of experience in coaching track and field. He was very successful in that sport. Coach Dick was of medium stature and had a heart of gold. He taught me how to high jump using the belly-roll style prior to the Fosbury Flop which came into use during the late sixties.

Coach Leonard Dick also taught me to pole-vault. Only bamboo poles were used. The pole's diameter was very large so it was difficult to get my hands around it. The landing pit was either sawdust or wood chips. Since Woodberry had an indoor track, I learned during the winter months. I did not play basketball until my junior year in 1953.

Estil and I built a pole vaulting pit beside Daddy's blacksmith shop. We had to haul in a lot of sawdust from the Martin sawmill in Lignum. We practiced vaulting after coming home from track practice, only if we had no farming chores to do. Coach Howard let us borrow a vaulting pole.

Culpeper County High School did not have a track so we ran around the football field. A jumping pit was built nearby so we had to find sawdust to put in it. We could not have a home track meet since we did not have a track. Our home meets were held at Woodberry Forest since they had outstanding athletic facilities. In fact, we had some meets against Coach Dick's track teams. It is interesting that I beat Coach Dick's high jumpers and pole-vaulters in those meets. He made it a point to congratulate me after the meets.

At one of the meets at Woodberry, I had a bamboo vaulting pole to break while I was pole-vaulting. I was blessed not to be hurt so I finished that competition by vaulting ten feet which set a school record for Culpeper County High School.

As a child, I got migraine headaches so bad that I would have to go to bed, even ending in vomiting. It took about twenty-four hours to run its course. While a freshman in high school, I got headaches often from studying and reading. Finally, Mama made a decision to send me to an optometrist to get my eyes checked. It was determined that I had very poor vision. In fact, I was nearsighted in my right eye and farsighted in my left eye. The doctor said, "If you had waited any longer, you may have had to use a seeing-eye-dog. You must wear your glasses all the time except when sleeping." I was fitted for glasses. I saw clearly for the first time in my life. Back at school, very few students said anything about my glasses. When I played football or participated in running sports, I did not wear glasses. In fact I saw fairly well in catching a ball or judging distances. For the first time in my life, I saw what was written on the chalk board. Also, my migraine headaches became less frequent. I never did thank Mama and Daddy for getting glasses for me. I needed to improve on being thankful for the many things that other people did for me.

Because I became quite interested in football and track, it motivated me to study hard in school. Coach Howard helped me since he knew my home situation, without a father and also not living with my mother. When I started dating in high school, he loaned me his car. Daddy had an old truck which wasn't very convenient to be used for a date, but I used it some.

During my junior year, the basketball coach Tom Young asked me to come out for the basketball team, which I knew little about. I could make lay-ups (snowbirds) and could play good defense since I had good speed. My long shots at the top of the circle were accurate only about forty percent of the time. The uniforms (especially the shorts which were very short and sometimes to the point of hurting) were a complete reversal of what is worn today. During that time, there were no "three points" plays and no dunking the ball allowed especially hanging on the rim like a monkey. During this year, I was a starter in football, basketball, and track. I was blessed to achieve much success in all three sports and lettered in all three. I really enjoyed them, perhaps taking out my frustrations in those sports. Also, I made the honor roll and was Chairman of the hall monitors, and President of the Hi-Y.

I really enjoyed my senior year of 1950-1951. Being motivated by Coach Howard and Mama, I strived to do better. I studied harder, also.

We had a very successful year in football, basketball, and track. One of the teams we played was Manassas High School which had a good team that year. The day of that game, I had an upset stomach and could not go to school. Coach Howard called Mama and asked why I wasn't in school. He told her I could not play that night if I wasn't in school, which were the school's rules. Mama gave me an aspirin and asked, "Do you feel like going to school?" I said, "Yes, ma'am." As the day progressed, I began to feel better. Perhaps my "butterflies" were bothering me too much. We beat Manassas that night 59-7. I had my best game ever and scored five touchdowns.

During Coach Howard's three previous seasons, his football team had quite a reputation. I was elected captain and Jug Payne was the alternate captain. The smaller schools with the same enrollment as ours, about four-hundred-fifty students, did not want to play us. We played teams of larger enrollments such as Mount Vernon, Woodward Prep, Highland Springs, Glen Allen (now Hermitage), Falls Church, and Fairfax. Whenever we played teams in our classification, we won and won many of the others.

During the basketball season, we had a successful year with Tom Young as our coach. We had a winning season and qualified for the state tournament held at Randolph Macon College in Ashland, Virginia. We won the first two games and then lost.

Right after Christmas, Coach Howard wanted to enter me in the high jump and sixty-yard-dash in the high school division at the Southern Conference (now Atlantic Coast Division) indoor track meet in Chapel Hill, North Carolina. The basketball coach Tom Young agreed to allow me to go to that meet since it required me to miss several basketball practices. I did not do well in the sixty-yard-dash (no medals), but I got second in the high jump at five-feet-nine-inches, a personal best. The athlete who won was from Highland Springs High School in Richmond Virginia.

Track season was very exciting and very tiring. I was elected captain and Ray Grady was elected alternate captain. In each meet, I ran the 100-yard-dash, 220-yard-dash, 880-relay anchor, high jump, pole-vault, broad jump, shot, and discus. During the Rappahannock Relays in Fredericksburg, I won three blue ribbons for first place, and three red ribbons for second place. I tied a CCHS record in the 100-yard-dash held by Sam Fray in a time of 10.2 seconds. The dash was run on grass which was roped off on the football field, at Maury Stadium in Fredericksburg, Virginia.

In 1951 the senior prom was held in the gymnasium. I had been dating Ann Graves for two years. We dated only on weekends since Mama made me study on nights before school. One of our house rules was to be home by ten o'clock at night which was also a rule for our football, basketball, and track coach, A.T. Howard. Since the prom was special and did not end until ten o'clock, I did not discuss with Mama what time I had to be home. When the prom ended, Ann invited several couples to her house for a party. At about eleven o'clock, I had a phone call from Mama asking, "Where are you? You know you are supposed to be home by ten!"

I said, "I'm at Ann's house with several other couples having a party."

She said, "I don't care what you are doing, I want you to come home now!"

"I will be there in a few minutes," I quickly replied.

We lived about five minutes away. Mama was waiting up for me and reminded me that my curfew was ten o'clock. She did not have harsh words for me.

There was a boy at the prom and party who obviously admired Ann. He began dating her soon after I left for college. During Christmas that year, Ann and I ended our relationship.

During my senior year, there were schools that wanted me to come on football scholarships. Some of those were the University of Virginia, the University of Maryland, the University of North Carolina, VMI and others. I wanted to go to a college where I knew that I would play or even be a starter as a freshman. The larger schools at that time were not allowed to start freshmen on the varsity team.

Coach Howard checked with some schools in the WVIAC (West Virginia Intercollegiate Athletics Conference). Coach took me to Shepherd College to talk to the coach. He told us that I was too small to play football for him. I was five-feet-nine and weighed one-hundred-seventy pounds. Next, we went to Concord College in Athens, West Virginia. The football coach, Joe Friedl, offered me a football scholarship and reminded me if I was good enough, I could start playing as a freshman.

Graduation day arrived in May, 1951. I was quite excited since I would be playing football next year as a freshman in college. I was fortunate enough to be selected as one of four outstanding seniors. The others were Jackie Kilby, Martha Ann Colvin, and Barry Hounshell. Also, I acquired school records in track in all field events (shot, discus, high jump, pole-vault, broad jump) and tied the record with Sam Fray with a time of 10.2 in the 100-yard-dash.

Coach Howard accepted a football head coaching position at Beaver High School in Bluefield, West Virginia, beginning in the fall of 1951. Coach Howard and I moved to Bluefield, West Virginia, which is about twenty miles from Concord College in Athens, West Virginia. He talked to my grandparents and my mother about legally adopting me. They agreed and in June he legally adopted me. I lived with him until football practice began at Concord. He got me a summer job at a car dealership in Bluefield working as a prep for washing and cleaning cars, which was a lot easier than working for Virginia Department of Highways. One day, I became careless in driving one of the vehicles from outside to inside and put a small dent in one of the fenders. I went to my boss and explained what had happened, thinking I would be fired. I told him that I would pay for it, but he told me that he had insurance to cover it. I remained working there until August when football practice began.

A short time after Coach Howard and I arrived in Bluefield, a birth certificate was obtained from the Census Bureau in Richmond, Virginia. I found out that my real birth name is Irvin Daniel Crane. Prior to that, I had been told that my name was Daniel Irving Crane. What a shock! Another big question in my mind! My high school diploma has Daniel Irving Crane and my college diploma has Irvin Daniel Crane.

Coach Howard's life was about football. When he left for WWII, he was engaged to a beautiful blond girl. She wanted to get married before he left for the war, but he did not want to do that in fear he would not return. Midway during his service in the war, he found out that she fell in love with someone else and married. It must have broken his heart since he never got engaged again. There is an old saying, "Absence makes the heart grow fonder...for someone else."

Coach A.T. Howard always took care of his

football players, even buying food and clothes for some. No one knows but Coach, how many football scholarships he got for his players including those for Stanley, Estil, and me.

After Coach Howard adopted me, I started calling him A.T. He was my adopted father from that time until he died at the age of forty-nine in 1965. He was the primary motivator in my life especially in high school, college, and at the beginning of my coaching career.

Chapter Five

My Fifth Earthly Angel, Coach Joe Friedl

Coach Joe Friedl was an athlete at Western Kentucky University and had been a high school coach in West Virginia prior to coming to Concord College in 1948. He started his first year at Concord as assistant football coach under the head coach Robert Kyle. Coach Friedl was a good coach, well versed in blocking and tackling, and quite a motivator. If a player made a great tackle or a running back made a long touchdown run, he would always pat a player on the back and say, "You could have done better." The football program from 1946-1950 was eleven wins, twenty-eight losses and three ties.

In 1951, Coach Friedl became the head football coach at Concord with Joseph Vachon as his assistant. This was my freshman year. The football program had not been very successful for a few years. Coach Friedl started a program by bringing in a lot of freshmen to build for the future. Many times, "Coach" started all freshmen players as he looked forward to the future. Needless to say, the team had a long season and only won one football game.

I was a starter at running back, safety, running back punts and kick-offs, and punting. My favorite play was off right tackle with the tackle being Don Williams and the end being Ray Halsey. Ray would put his hand on his butt to show which way he was blocking the defensive end, so I could run the opposite way. If he blocked the end inside, I would run to the outside and if he blocked the end outside, I would run inside. We had good results.

Halfway through the season, a visiting team arrived on Friday afternoon and it began snowing. Concord College was built on a high hill so the wind blew most of the time. I told people back home in Virginia that it snowed parallel to the ground at Concord. By Saturday morning, the snow had accumulated almost one foot. The game had to start at two o'clock in the afternoon since the visiting team had arrived the night before. Both teams enjoyed playing in the snow. Every time we got tackled or we tackled someone, we slid for many yards. It was almost like being a kid and going sledding. On one of the plays our quarterback, Tom Atwell, called play number 36-Crane off right tackle. There was a huge opening so I ran there, as Ray had given me the signal. I met a defensive back and with a little fake in one direction I went the other way. It was funny watching players slip and fall as I went untouched for ninety-two yards for a touchdown. It was the longest touchdown run that I had ever made, even including high school.

Later that year, our team went to play Morris

Harvey College in Charleston, West Virginia. They had an experienced football team and they were ranked nationally. We started all freshmen and they had mostly seniors. We got beat 56-0. I played sixty minutes in that game and was beaten physically, the worst beaten I've ever had. The next day, it was difficult to walk or move although I was in great physical condition.

Coach Friedl was also head basketball coach. One day he said, "Danny, I want you to come out for basketball after football season."

I told him, "I played only two years of high school basketball."

He said, "I want you on the team because of your quickness and speed."

"I am not a very good basketball player," I responded.

I agreed to go out for the team. Toward the end of my first practice he said, "Danny, I want to see you in my office after practice."

I said, "Yes, sir."

When I got in his office he said, "Danny, you are right, you are not a very good basketball player." I did not say anything. His last statement to me before I left was, "But you are an excellent football player. Stick with it!"

In February of 1952, A.T. encouraged me to enter the high jump at the Southern Conference Indoor Track meet at the University of North Carolina in Chapel Hill. I did not have a place to work-out so I was hesitant. We went to that meet. I participated in the high jump in the College Freshman Division. Leonard Muse from the

University of Virginia and I tied for firs[t]
leap of six-feet-zero inches which was a[...]
for me.

After football season in the spr[ing]
Randy Snyder and I wanted to go to the V[...]
Track Meet. We did not have a track team[...]
so we asked our Athletic Director, Charles "[...]
if he could enter us in the meet. He told us[...]
and he would take us. We practiced with A.T[...]
track team at Beaver High School in Bluef[ield]
Virginia. Randy threw the shot and discus.[...]
100- yard dash, high jump, broad jump, and p[...]
In the WVIAC meet, Randy won the shot put a[nd]
the long jump. I also placed in the other fiel[d]
Randy and I placed in the top score for third place.

In the summer of 1952, A.T. got me a summer
job working for the Norfolk and Western Railroad
Company. Mr. "Beef" Smith hired me because he
wanted me to play fast pitch softball with the N&W team
at Bluefield, West Virginia. We could not play softball
for them unless we were an employee. At work, my
job was to help repair the brakes on trains. We traveled
to several states, naturally by train, to play softball. I
played short-stop and batted first because Coach Smith
wanted me to run the bases since I was fast. We had a
good record until we went to Portsmouth, Ohio, to play
in a national tournament. Their pitcher could throw a
softball faster than any pitcher that I have ever seen.
The speed was not measured, but all of our players had
a hard time even seeing the ball as it left the pitcher's
hand. Needless to say, we lost the game. We learned

the lesson that there is always someone who is "better than you"!

In late August of 1952, my sophomore year, we began football practice. One morning, I awoke with severe pain in my stomach. As the day went on, the pain got worse and worse. Coach Friedl called A.T. and very soon he came to take me to the hospital in Bluefield, West Virginia. I had an appendicitis attack, so surgery was performed a few hours later. I was really depressed that I would not be able to play football that year, another disappointment in my life. Athletics had been my motivation up to this point in my life.

The surgery was performed by Dr. Bob Gatherum, a friend of A.T. 's. The healing process progressed nicely and I began to feel better. I asked Dr. Bob if it were possible for me to play in a few football games. At that time, an eight semester rule applied so we could not have an extra year to play. After four weeks of healing, I felt like playing. Dr. Gatherum said he could make me a plastic pad to be used over the incision for protection. A.T. did not want me to play. He had a talk with Dr. Bob and they agreed that I could play the last three games of the season but I could play only defense. That way, I would not be exposed to being tackled. He said I could also run back punts. After only one week of practice for me, our team went to play West Liberty College. During the second quarter, I was running back a punt. Three defenders were bearing down on me. In order to protect myself, I stepped out-of-bounds on the sidelines. As I did, I was hit by all three defenders. I saw stars, moons, suns, lightning, satellites, and comets…all at one time. I got up to start back to the bench and collapsed. I woke up several hours after the game ended. After that, Coach Friedl did not want me to play much in the next two games. It was a very long, trying, disappointing time for me, another setback.

After football season, I exercised daily by running on my own and playing indoor handball. Coach Bob Kyle, our P.E. teacher and strict disciplinarian, taught me how to play handball. Our handball court was only a two-wall handball court. He was a very rough player so I was glad it was not four walls or he would have killed me! I played with him every chance I had so I would become better. Once in awhile I would beat him, claiming to be the only student who could beat him. One year, I won the championship in intramural handball.

Spring of 1953 found me wanting to go to the WVIAC track and field meet in Ogleby Park in Wheeling, West Virginia. Concord still did not have a track team. Coach Baxter agreed to take me so I once again worked out at Beaver High School with A.T. Howard's track team. Randy Snyder had graduated so I entered the meet by myself. Once again, I high jumped, broad jumped, pole-vaulted, and ran the 100-yard-dash. That day I set the WVIAC pole-vault record at eleven-feet-six-inches using a Swedish steel vaulting pole and landing in sawdust. I was the leading scorer in the meet. Coach Baxter informed me that if I won the mile run, our college could win the meet. Since I had not trained for that event and was tired, I told him that I could not do that. I did not participate in track anymore until I participated in the Armed Forces meet in Germany in

1956.

Our football team did quite well that fall with a record of four wins, three losses and one tie. I was still playing running back, left safety, and ran back kick-offs and punts. I played sixty minutes unless we got so far ahead that subs could play or if we got hurt. That was the year we got plastic helmets with suspensions inside. After being hit or hitting someone very hard (we could hit them with the helmets at that time) my ears would ring for several seconds. I wanted my old leather helmet back, but it was not allowed. Face masks and mouth pieces were still not being used.

I had the most success that year in football that I had ever had. Our offensive line had improved and they opened many holes for the backs to run through. That year, I was selected on the first team squad on the West Virginia Intercollegiate Athletic Conference team. Jim Miles, offensive guard and nose guard, was also selected on the first team.

The highlight of that season for me was a game with West Virginia Tech in Beckley, West Virginia, in the King Cole Bowl. A.T. told me that the coach there had been the coach at Shepherd College, the one who had told me that I was too small to play for him. I was so motivated that I couldn't wait for the game to start. I wanted to prove to him that I wasn't too small to play for him or anyone else.

West Virginia Tech had a good sound football team. During the game our quarterback, Tom Atwell called play 36-Crane off right tackle, my favorite play. I had a great opening, made a cutback and ran seventy-five yards for a touchdown. When I looked back down the field, I saw that our offensive lineman had been off-sides! When I got back to the huddle, Tom asked me if I could run the same play again. I told him I was tired, but would try. I could not believe that gaping hole was there again, so I ran eighty yards for a touchdown. That was the highlight of my football career. I went on to score two other touchdowns that game. We won the game by one touchdown.

In 1954, Stubby Currance, sports director at the Bluefield Daily Telegraph, always gave Concord good publicity. Whenever I set a conference football record, he had a write-up about it. A.T., who was coaching at Beaver High School, also got good coverage. Since Stubby knew that A.T. was my legal guardian, he was especially good to me even if I had a bad game. Many times in his articles he would refer to me as "The Concord Express," "Dashing Danny," or "Danny Boy." I got a lot of kidding about that! Stubby was very instrumental in getting me named to the WVIAC first team my junior and senior years and also getting me named to the first team on the NAIA football team my senior year.

When football practice began my senior year, I was very excited because I had a great year as a junior. I set several WVIAC records and had been selected to the first team All-WVIAC. Since I had been captain of the football team and track team in high school, I felt that I should be captain of our football team in college. To my dismay, when the team voted, I was not chosen. Tom Atwell, quarterback, and Jim Miles, right guard, were chosen. Another big disappointment occurred in my life. I felt defeated and really had a problem handling that situation. I thought about quitting the team, but continued practicing. When the weekend arrived, I went to see A.T. and explained what had happened. Once again, my earthly angel gave me sound advice. He said, "It would be very selfish for you to quit the team since you're on a football scholarship." The best advice he gave me was, "This incident can be a motivation for you to be the best football player Concord has ever had." I went back to the team and worked my butt off and had a great season.

Coach Friedl was a soft-spoken coach who made a player want to get better with each game. He did not overwork us, but was a very clever coach. When a player came off the field during a game, he gave encouragement whether the ball was fumbled, a tackle missed, or a touchdown scored. He took an interest in each player; it did not matter if the player was a third stringer. It was a pleasure playing for him.

I had my best football season that year, leading the WVIAC in several categories: rushing one-thousand-twelve yards and averaging eight yards per carry. I was named first string running back that year. Teams then only played eight games per year. We only had about thirty players on our football team. Many of us had to play both offense and defense. We did not have rotating fans with a mist to cool us off, or stationary bicycles to ride as they do today. We were taught to be tough.

My senior year was exciting for our football team as we had played together for three years. We were all striving to win the WVIAC championship. We worked extremely hard in the preseason practices. With the encouragement of our quarterback, Tom, some of us stayed after practice to run more plays and to run some extra wind sprints. We won many games and qualified to play Morris Harvey College, a football powerhouse, for the WVIAC championship title. They had a running back, "Gummy" Carr, a great athlete. I was pretty good at tackling, but when "Gummy" Carr broke open down the sidelines and I hit him with all my strength, I bounced off and he went on to score a touchdown. After graduation, he played for the (then called) St. Louis Cardinals for several years. Morris Harvey beat us 25-7 with me only scoring one touchdown. That team was not only very talented but they were also very hard tacklers and blockers.

That year I set several WVIAC records and led the conference in several categories. I was named captain of the All-WVIAC team. It was sad knowing that all of us would never get together as a team again, but many of us remained friends for a long time.

After the season, I found out that I had been named to the first team NAIA All-American Football team, the first All-American football player at Concord College. I began receiving letters from several professional football teams. I filled out the questionnaire forms and sent them back. Several months later, I received a football contract from the Pittsburg Steelers for $4,500. At that time, they only played for three months. I had to make a decision to accept or reject the contract. I spent a lot of time talking to A.T. about it...to accept or reject. A.T. told me that he thought I could make it but said, "What happens if you get a serious injury?" I was five-feet-nine inches tall and only weighed one-hundred-seventy-five pounds, but I was fast, had good hands, and could block and tackle. While I was waiting to decide, I was notified by the draft board that I would be inducted into the Army in August of 1955 so I could not accept the contract. I thought that my football playing days were over.

Saying goodbye to Coach Friedl was a sad time. While I was playing for him I looked up to him as a substitute father since A.T. was in Bluefield and I was in Athens. Although A.T. attended most of our games, he never tried to coach me while I was playing college football. He congratulated me on several occasions when I played an exceptional game.

Several years later Coach Friedl was instrumental in getting me named to the All-Time Football Team and the All-Time Track Team for the state of West Virginia. It is interesting that I only participated in two conference track meets since Concord did not have a track team in 1951-1955!

Chapter Six

My Sixth Earthly Angel, Maxine Weaver Crane

On August 1, 1955, I was inducted into the army at Fort Jackson, South Carolina. After going through all the physicals, including a G.I. haircut, I took a battery of tests. The results showed that I qualified to attend Officers' Candidate School. After learning that it would require four years in the military as an officer as compared to two years if I remained a private, I decided not to become an officer. I wanted to get back into sports as soon as possible, which was my life. After several days of indoctrination, our unit was transferred to the Third Armored Division at Fort Knox, Kentucky.

Basic training was quite interesting, especially watching and following our Drill Sergeant who was yelling commands. Since I enjoyed jogging, I looked forward to our running whereas some recruits could not keep up the pace. They constantly received a berating from the Drill Sergeant.

After the third day, several military officers came to where we were training. They were football coaches for the Fort Knox team "looking for Danny Crane."

One of the coaches asked me, "Would you like to play football for one of our teams at Fort Knox?"

I immediately said, "When can I start?"

The coach said, "You must be timed in the 40-yard-dash first."

"When can I do it?" I asked.

He said, "Right now."

With my heavy combat boots on, I was timed. After completing the sprint, one of them said, "Come with me!" I went to be fitted with a football uniform. I couldn't believe that I was going to play army football.

I had not completed basic training yet, so on Saturdays I had to qualify by shooting the M1 rifle, crawling the infiltration course, and going through the gas chamber with a gas mask. Several of the other soldiers seemed quite envious that I was given special treatment.

We had former football players from various colleges and universities on the team such as West Virginia, Rice, Michigan, West Liberty, South Carolina, North Carolina, Glenville, and Alabama. We also had professional players on the team since they had been drafted into the United States Army.

Our team was very good that year. I became a starter at running back and at defensive back. I also returned punts and kick-offs. The third game began with me running back a kick-off. When tackled, I felt pain in my right arm. I did not tell the coach until after the game. I was afraid that he would not let me play anymore in the game. After telling him and showing him my swollen arm, I was taken to the hospital for X-rays. My ulna, the small bone in the lower arm, was broken. A cast was put on my arm. I asked the doctor if I could still play football. He said, "Maybe your coach and I can work out something." After talking to the coach, he said that I could play but would have to cover the cast with thick rubber. Man, was I happy! I played the rest of the season and had a good season. I used the cast on my arm as a weapon!

While in the United States Army in Fort Knox and later while stationed in Germany, I got very little mail from home. One of my cousins, Patsy Brown (daughter of Edith and Roy Brown) was very faithful in writing letters to me. She really encouraged me and kept me aware of what was going on at home. She wrote entertaining letters and had a great sense of humor. In fact, she is still a talented writer. She has published many articles from her current home in Bedford, Pennsylvania.

During that fall, I learned that my football jersey, number 28, was going to be retired at Concord College. It would be the first one to be retired there. Frank Parker, my roommate at Concord for two years and fraternity brother of Phi Delta Pi, had been instrumental in getting that done. I was invited to Concord's homecoming to participate in the ceremony but could not go because we had a game that day. Jersey number 28, with all of my football accomplishments, was framed and placed in the gym lobby in the trophy case.

In the spring of 1956, our army unit was getting ready to be shipped to Germany to a small base at Butzbach. It was located about twenty miles from

Frankfurt. The trip across the Atlantic Ocean by ship was relatively smooth but became quite rough when we sailed through the North Sea. After nine days, we landed at Bremerhaven Port and took a train to our base. It was a beautiful country. I enjoyed seeing the German terrain of flora and fauna. When we arrived at the base, we discovered that our sleeping and living accommodations were in an old stately but dilapidated castle.

Football began in August of 1956 and I was called from my unit to get equipped with a football uniform. I found out that I would be in Special Services during the season, away from my company. Our football schedule allowed us to travel and to play other U.S. military teams in places such as Frankfurt, Berlin, Heidelberg, Munich, and other places. Our team consisted of some players that I had played against in college and several pro-football players. Our quarterback Lieutenant Ted Anderson was also one of our coaches. He played quarterback for West Virginia University in the Sugar Bowl prior to this time.

Our army team played for the division championship and lost by one touchdown. I had a good season and made one of the All-Army teams.

After our game in Berlin, Germany, several football players and I went to a nightclub there. Each table had its own telephone with large 1, 2, or 3 digit numbers. When we saw a beautiful Fraulein, we dialed a number for conversation. That was in 1956, probably the forerunner of cell phones.

On the way back to our base, we found that we

had wandered into the Eastern sector of Berlin. When we tried to leave, we were arrested. We were detained for several hours before our coach came and verified that we were not spies but football players from Butzbach. Later the Berlin wall was removed under President Ronald Reagan when he said, "Take down that wall."

While in Germany, I began to backslide as a Christian. I did not go to church, did not pray, and did not write to my family. I was questioning God on why I had no one close to me to understand my life without a Father and without a Mother. Because of my success as an athlete, I felt like I did not need the Lord. I began smoking cigarettes and started drinking German beer, although I would not do those things when playing sports. I went from 175 pounds to 195 pounds causing me to lose some speed, although I remained faster than most others.

While in the army, my birth mother became ill with rheumatoid arthritis and could work no longer. Her medical bills were so high (surgeries on her fingers, toes, back, knee, and neck) that I had to send half of my paycheck to her in Virginia to help pay expenses. It was during that time that my older stepsister, Peggy, had to learn to cook, clean, wash, etc, and to help raise her younger sister, Joan. My stepfather, Clyde, worked for the Virginia Department of Highways nine-and-one-half hours a day so he was not able to help out too much at home.

On December 15, I learned that my mother was very ill with rheumatoid arthritis and that she "might not live much longer." I was given a leave of two weeks to fly to Virginia to see her. With the pay of a Specialist I, I could not afford the trip to the states. The army and Red Cross paid my expenses for me to fly home. When arriving in Virginia, I stayed with Daddy and Mama in Lagrange. I went to see my birth mother who was in the hospital. After several days, she had a remarkable recovery and went home.

The second night home, I called a high school friend, Maxine Weaver, for a date. She turned out to be the best earthly angel I've had. I said to Maxine, "How are you doing?"

"Where are you?" she inquired.

I told her all about my flight back to the states and then said, "I heard that you are engaged. Is that correct?"

She hesitated and then replied, "Not really."

I said, "Would you like to go on a date with me?"

She accepted and we had a wonderful time together. She was a very kind, compassionate, understanding, and vivacious person. We dated several times before I went back to Germany.

When I got back to Germany, I tried out for the All-European Track Meet to be held in the Berlin Stadium where Jesse Owens set a world record in the 100-yard-dash in 1936. We did not have a track team so I practiced on my own for the 100-meter-dash, javelin, and pole-vault.

It was the toughest competition in track that I have ever faced. I performed my personal best in each event but did not win any medals. My best event there was the 100-meter-dash, which qualified me for the finals in that event. It was won by Ira Murchinson who ran 10.5, a new record for that meet. (Later that year in the Olympics, he ran the anchor leg of the 400-meter-relay team which won a gold metal for the United States with record time.) I ran my personal best at 10.8 but finished behind Ira by about three meters. I found out what speed really is. It was a great experience running on the same track that Jesse Owens had set a world record and had become such a hero for many people, although Adolf Hitler would not pay any attention to him.

In the spring of 1957, our division prepared to return to the United States. I was scheduled to be discharged in May of that year. On the ship home, the ocean was very rough most of the way. Many of us became so sick that we could not eat for a couple of days. All of us were proud to see the "Statue of Liberty" again. My military days were very enjoyable and I considered remaining in the army but decided I wanted to go into teaching and coaching.

When I got back home, I told Mama that I had taken up the habit of smoking. I feared that she would punish me! She told me that I was old enough to smoke if I wanted but not to smoke around her (which I never did!) I was afraid to tell her that I had also started drinking beer. At times, I felt like drinking beer was an escape for me from my loneliness. I never thought of becoming an alcoholic, but did become a chain smoker...three packs a day!

As soon as I got back in Virginia, I called Maxine

again. We began dating. She had graduated that year from Catawba College in Salisbury, North Carolina.

In the meantime, A.T. got me a job at Central Junior High School in Bluefield, West Virginia. My salary would be $2,500 for the year. Two years prior to that the Pittsburg Steelers offered me $4,500 to play football for them!

Since I would not start teaching until August, I stayed in LaGrange. I found a summer job with Moore, Kelly, and Reddish Construction Company. My main job was driving heavy equipment from one site to another. Also, I drove the huge roller that pressed asphalt. One day, I drove the roller too far over the shoulder of the road. I thought that it would turn over so I stopped it and jumped off. Mr. Coleman, my boss said, "You get back on that roller and drive it back on the pavement." I said, "Yes, sir!" I did and everything was cool again. In fact, at the end of the summer, he wanted me to stay with the company, but athletics was on my mind, my true motivation in life.

That summer, Maxine and I dated many times and had great times together. I fell in love with her although I knew that I was going to be in Bluefield and she was going to be in Richmond, Virginia, teaching her first year at Bainbridge Junior High School. We decided to write to each other while we were separated. We courted by mail for one year.

While teaching at Central Junior High, I had a homeroom and five classes of physical science. I also was athletic director, head football coach, assistant basketball coach, and head track coach. In homeroom,

I had to teach spelling and penmanship. What irony! I had failed penmanship in college. In college I studied to be a teacher. One of the requirements was to pass penmanship. All we had to do was write cursively from a typed paragraph. I failed it two times with only two weeks left before graduation. When I went in the third time to pass the penmanship test, the professor said, "Danny Crane, you have failed this test two times and I know you will fail it again! Get out of here. I am going to pass you." Apparently, he was partial to football players. I told my seventh graders the whole story and they laughed about it. I used a lot of pictures on the board and told them how to practice capital letters and lower case letters. They did much better than I.

Prior to Christmas in 1957, I sent Maxine a telegram stating, "Have ring, will travel." I had purchased a diamond ring and was going to ask her to marry me. We went out to eat, then went to my cousin Sammy Crane's house. While there I proposed to Maxine and she accepted. Later we set a marriage date for August 9, 1958.

In the spring of 1958, I had a call from Emory Davis, athletic director and head football coach at Greensville County High School in Emporia, Virginia. He offered me a position as physical education teacher, assistant football coach, assistant basketball coach, head baseball coach, and head track coach. The only way that I could be both head baseball coach and head track coach was that track practice was held during physical education class and baseball practice was held after school. My salary would be $3,500. In my conversation with Maxine, I told her about the job so she applied as an English teacher. She got the job with a salary of $2,800 for the year. She signed a contract to teach English, history, music appreciation, and to direct the school choir.

In the summer of 1958, I went to live with Mama and Daddy in LaGrange. I got a job that summer tearing down the bowling alley in Culpeper, Virginia. It was the dirtiest job I have ever had.

Maxine and I dated frequently, and she did a lot of planning for our wedding at the Culpeper Baptist Church where Maxine was a member. I was still a member of Hopewell Methodist Church in Lignum, Virginia. The church had an outgoing pastor, Dr. Frank Cale, and an incoming pastor, Rev. John Farrar. She chose to have both pastors to perform the wedding. I believe she had two ministers so one could perform the ceremony and one would keep me from running away!

Mrs. Weaver was quite busy planning the wedding with Maxine. I spent a lot of time listening to them planning. Mr. Weaver said that he was constantly handing out money! About two weeks before the wedding, Mrs. Weaver asked me, "I'll bet you would like to be on a slow boat to China about now, wouldn't you?"

I replied, "No, Ma'am, I'd like to be on a fast boat to China!" We all got a good laugh about that.

A.T. served as best man for the wedding. All went well in the formal ceremony until I stepped on Maxine's gown as we went up three steps. I envisioned the gown falling off. She looked at me and smiled, so I knew everything would be all right.

Tommy Thompson sang the Lord's Prayer during the ceremony. Maxine chose him to sing, not only because he was a good friend in high school, but also because he sang on a local radio station WCVA in Culpeper on Saturdays and Maxine always played the piano for him.

The ceremony finally ended and we had a beautiful reception at the Weaver home. Many guests were there. After we ran through a downpour of rice, we headed to Skyline Drive for our honeymoon.

At the end of August, we moved to Emporia into a little four-room rental house at 416 Watkins Street. The rooms were large with a kitchen, a living room, two bedrooms and a bath. The rent was sixty dollars a month. We were happy as two bugs in a rug.

After the first year of teaching in Greensville County High School, we found out that we were going to have our first child. At that time, the school system would not let any teacher who was pregnant be on the staff. Since Maxine was pregnant, we would have only one salary of $3,900 for the following year. Bill Overbey and I applied to do summer work for the school system. We were hired to do maintenance work for all the schools including the white and Negro schools. Most of our work included painting the inside of schools and also painting the outdoor toilets. Bill had such a wit about him that I enjoyed his company although the work was not pleasant. It helped Maxine and me to survive.

On March 22, 1959, Mama Brown died. I recalled at that time the number of times I had given her injections to help relieve her asthmatic condition. I had lost my first angel and knew that she would be missed by many people, especially by Daddy and me. It was the first time I had seen Daddy cry.

On January 7, 1960, Maxine went to the Medical College of Virginia in Richmond, Virginia, to have our first baby. She was in labor for forty-two hours while I walked the halls in the hospital. Maxine almost gave up, but with help and surgery, Cheryl Danielle, finally arrived. When Dr. Ware came to announce her birth, I almost fainted with relief. What an ordeal!

In the spring of 1960, A.T. Howard was hired as the head coach of football at Gar-Field High School in Woodbridge, Virginia. Several years before that, he was instructed to stop coaching because he had a heart condition. He was released by Dr. Gatherum to start back into coaching. He called and asked me to be his assistant football coach. I was also offered the head track coach. Maxine was offered a job teaching English and Journalism and producing the school paper, "Indian Scripts."

After coaching a game of football with A.T. on November 9, 1961, we got the news that Daddy Brown had passed away. The family waited until after the game to tell A.T. and me. We both cried together. Daddy died during that afternoon. A.T. had spent a lot of time with Daddy and Mama and he was considered one of the family. It was one of the many sad times in my life. I had lost my second earthly angel, but his memory still lingers.

On October 10, 1962, our second daughter,

Catherine Michelle, was born at Mary Washington Hospital in Fredericksburg, Virginia. The birth was a lot easier than the first according to what Maxine told me. We had decided to have a second child since I wanted a boy, a future football player. The Lord knew what He was doing. If I had a son who wasn't a football player and track athlete, I probably would have broken his plate at every meal!

In 1962, we bought our first home in Gar-Field Estates for $13,900. It was conveniently located about two-hundred yards from Gar-Field High School. It was a three-bedroom rambler with a full basement and a large backyard. My Concord roommate Frank Parker, his wife Sarah, and their two children Danny and Sissy, moved next door to us. There were several other teachers who owned homes in that area. We enjoyed their company and friendship throughout our tenure at Gar-Field. That fall A.T. was offered a head coaching position at Fauquier County High School, the consolidation of Warrenton High School, Cedar Lee High School, and Marshall High School. He accepted the job. After he left, I became athletic director, head football coach, and head track coach at Gar-Field for the new school year of 1963.

Our girls hated to see him go. He had a bedroom with us and he was their grandfather, their playmate, their spoiler. Whatever they wanted, he got it for them.

A.T. was a great high school football coach not only because of his strict discipline but also because he knew how to teach the techniques of blocking and tackling. One day during August two-a-day practices,

Red Raines, another assistant football coach, and I decided to go to Manassas, Virginia, to play golf between practices. At about the fourteenth hole, I told Red that we had better head back so we would not be late for practice. He said that we had time to finish all eighteen holes. Guess what? We were about thirty minutes late. A.T. did not let us practice and informed us that we had to sit on the sidelines. In fact, he made us sit on the sidelines for several days before allowing us to coach again. We learned that we would not be late to practice anymore. In fact, we were the first at practice every day from then on.

Our whole family loved A.T. and he taught us many important lessons in life.

Chapter Seven

My Seventh Earthly Angel, Elton Weaver

Elton Weaver, my father-in-law, was my last earthly angel. If I had a choice as to whom to pick for a Father, it would have been him. He was about six-feet-tall and weighed about one-hundred-seventy-five pounds. Although he was not a very large man, he had a big heart. He was a fine Christian man of the Baptist faith. He owned a Gulf Station and the Culpeper Motor Court in Culpeper, Virginia. As time went on, I became more impressed with his unwavering character. After knowing Maxine for several years, I knew that he had to be a great father.

After Maxine and I moved closer to Culpeper, our family of four went to the Weaver home to spend almost every weekend and to celebrate Christmas there, also. Mr. Weaver and I did many things together such as hunting, fishing, and farming. After the death of his mother, he bought his siblings' share of their one-hundred-fifty-acre farm in Madison County where he grew up.

One year he and I went into the Black Angus

cattle business. We harvested hay, and raised corn (cutting it by hand, shocking it, shucking it by hand and putting it in the corn house.) We also had a big garden. One year we dug twenty-five bushels of potatoes, plus harvesting other vegetables. He did not live on that farm and neither did I. We were farmers who lived away from the farm.

We were at the farm one day and he was mowing hay using a tractor with a long cutting blade. I asked, "Would you teach me how to mow hay like that?"

He said, "Yes, but I have to show you how. I will stand on the back of the tractor and tell you what to do."

"Won't that be dangerous?"

"I will be careful," he responded. .

Shortly after I put the mower in action, I heard him yell. His brand new bibbed overalls had caught in the pitman rod which rotates back and forth and it was twisting the overalls around his leg. I stopped the tractor instantly and cut off the engine. After getting him freed from the rod, I said, "I'm going to take you to a doctor!"

He said, "I don't need to see a doctor."

I couldn't see the full damage to the leg but I said, "You have a bad injury so I am going to take you!"

Sure enough the leg was broken. The doctor put a cast on his leg. I felt bad that I had caused him to break his leg. Later, he told me that he should not have been standing on the back of the tractor while I was mowing.

One of the things Mr. Weaver taught me was to

hunt deer. He belonged to the Rapidan Rod and Gun Club in Richardsville, Virginia, in the eastern part of Culpeper County. At this time dogs could be used for hunting. He invited me as a guest to go to the club and "deer hunt" one Thanksgiving morning. To begin the hunt, we were organized into standers and drivers. The standers were spaced about one-hundred yards apart at the edge of the woods. I was a stander that day. The drivers lined up on the opposite side of the woods about seventy to one-hundred yards apart. They walked in a straight line and yelled loudly to chase the deer toward the standers. It seemed dangerous to me. Luckily, no one was shot. At that time, only shotguns could be used and only buckshot number zero could be used. Rifle hunting was allowed several years later. During the drive, I shot at a deer about one-hundred yards away but missed, not knowing that buckshot would not travel that far. I was so disappointed especially knowing that if a club member missed a deer, the custom was to cut off his shirttail at the end of the day.

Later that same morning, each hunter was put out in the woods in certain areas. I was located about one-hundred yards off a dirt road. Some members had dogs that would chase deer. The reason for the drivers was to drive deer to hunters to be shot and to get the deer moving to produce trails for the dogs to follow.

Just to my back across the dirt road, I heard the hounds running. They kept getting closer and closer. Mr. Weaver had just told me to wait until deer get as close as fifty yards before shooting. I turned and saw two deer circling to my left about one-hundred yards away. My heart was beating about one-hundred times per minute as the adrenalin was flowing fast. The two deer turned to my right and stopped about forty yards from me. The lead deer was the larger of the two so I pointed my twelve gauge shotgun loaded with double-ought-buck. As the trigger caused the ammunition to leave the gun, I thought I had missed. To my surprise, both of the deer (does) fell to the ground "deader than a door nail." I became so excited that I yelled, "I have killed two deer with one shot and do not know what to do" The hunting law at that time was that a hunter could kill only one deer a day, and that only one doe could be killed during the season. If a second deer was killed, it had to be a buck.

A hunter came to where I was and asked what had happened. He said, "I only heard one shot" which is what I had done. He said, "Do not worry about what you did. I will claim one and you claim the other."

Since Mama Brown and my Sunday School teacher Frances taught me to always tell the truth, I said, "That is not the way it happened."

The game warden, Harmon Robinson, was a member of the hunt club and happened to be at the club that day. A hunter went to find him and brought him to the now "group of hunters" surrounding the two dead deer. Mr Robinson asked me, "What happened? Are you sure you shot only one time."

I said, "Yes, sir!"

He asked, "Are there any witnesses to that?" Two hunters spoke up and said, "Yes!"

Mr. Robinson said that I had broken two laws that

day…killing two deer in one day, and killing two does in one season. He said, "I do not know what to do!" After several minutes of thinking the situation over, he said, "I will have to give you a summons to appear in court and ban you from hunting until further notice."

"That is not fair," I replied. "It was an accident. If I am going to court, I want to see the judge right now."

Mr. Robinson agreed to do so. After going through all of that, I guess the club members forgot about cutting off my shirttail. After field dressing the deer, with the help of other hunters, we put both deer in the trunk of the game warden's car and headed to Culpeper to Judge Ream's house. On the way, we stopped at the convict camp and gave them one deer, the smaller of the two. I guess they had Thanksgiving dinner at my expense.

Mr. Robinson and I arrived at the home of Judge Reams where he had just sat down to eat his Thanksgiving dinner. Mr. Robinson went into the house and explained to the judge what happened. They came outside where I was waiting and Judge Reams said, "Tell me what happened." I told him the whole story . After listening intently, he said, "Danny Crane, I remember you in high school as an honor student and as an outstanding athlete. I know that you have never been in trouble with the law." He continued, "Since it was an accident, I am not going to fine you nor take your hunting license away. But, when you go back to hunting, you make sure that the next deer you kill will have at least twelve points on the rack and weigh two-hundred pounds."

I was so relieved and said, "Thank you, sir. I will

be more careful in the future." From that moment on I became a deer hunter. Later I joined the Rapidan Rod and Gun Club and hunted very successfully many times with Mr. Weaver. He taught me how to enjoy nature even if we did not see any deer. He had a tremendous outlook on life, always positive in every situation.

The years 1959-1965 were times of sadness for me since Mama Brown died in 1959, Daddy Brown died in 1961, Clyde died in 1961, my mother died in 1964, and A.T. died in 1965. During those times, Mr. Weaver seemed to take more interest in me. We did more fatherly things together. Since I never grew up with a father, I was really challenged about being a Father to my two girls. I was blessed that they had a good Mother to take up the slack when I did not know what to do. In my teaching and coaching, I tried to help those students and athletes who were having family problems.

When Maxine's mother and father visited us in Woodbridge, we always attended Calvary Baptist Church which was in the Gar-Field subdivision. Mr. Weaver loved our pastor's preaching. Rev Anthony Cunio was a miniature Billy Graham. A converted Catholic, he gave great sermons. We became close friends. Other Christian friends there were Ray and Eloise Tolson whose sons Ray and Robbie played football for me at Gar-Field High School. The Tolsons, the Cunios, and the Cranes got together and played the game of Rook quite often. At our house one night, we took a break from the game and had dessert. I said to Pastor Cunio, "Would you like a cup of coffee?"

"No, thank you, I am a Christian."

I was dumbfounded! I responded, "You mean Christians can't drink coffee?"

He gave his little chuckle and said, "I was just kidding."

Calvary Baptist Church was a large part of our lives in the 60's. Maxine played the piano for the Sunday morning service and for the choir. Alma Cunio, the pastor's wife, played the organ. The Cunios were such a happy couple. Pastor Cunio always joked about their relationship. One Sunday in the middle of a sermon he said, "I am the head of the house." Then he looked over and smiled at Alma and said, "And she's the neck that turns the head."

I sat next to Ray Tolson in the choir and sang whatever he sang. Our choir director Art Crane (no relation) was a U.S. Marine stationed at Quantico. He selected beautiful Christmas and Easter cantatas for us to sing. One year our Easter cantata was performed at the Lorton Prison. That was quite an experience as we watched the inmates file in with their issued clothes of black and white stripes. They were very receptive to our singing the gospel message.

Sunday nights were wonderful Christian experiences at Calvary Baptist Church. It was a different service from the formal Sunday morning service. It was usually a time of singing favorite hymns and giving testimonies. Pastor Cunio started the service with hymn requests. Every time he asked for requests, Cathie held up her hand. From the age of five, her favorite was "The Old Rugged Cross." When her hand went up, Pastor Cunio would always say, "Yes, Cathie, I know it's page sixty-six."

Sometimes Cathie sat on the front row with her little boyfriend. They were about six years old when I decided to deter little Danny Bausbaum's arm from being around her shoulders. He loved to twirl her long blond hair around his fingers. After service one night, I told Cathie that she would have to stop that behavior in church. She looked up at me with those big brown eyes and said, "Don't worry Daddy, I won't get married until I'm thirteen."

The Weavers celebrated Christmas at our house. One Christmas Eve they were babysitting with the girls while Maxine and I were at church. Cheryl and Cathie loved Barbie dolls and had so many, that one bedroom was converted into a "Barbie Room." They were playing dolls, when a knock was heard at the front door. Mrs. Weaver went to the door. There was Santa Claus! He came in and went straight to the recreation room. He said, "Where are Maxine and Danny?"

Mrs. Weaver said, "They're at church."

Santa looked all around, inquired about the girls, and then he left.

When we got home from church, Mrs. Weaver couldn't wait to tell us all about the mysterious "Santa." I immediately went to the phone and called neighbors and friends to see who came to visit. I also called the police to ask about a strange Santa Claus. No one had seen "Santa." To this day, we do not know who visited.

For years we speculated on who came into our house. Our superstitious nature said that it was probably A.T. since we always smelled his pipe tobacco at Christmas!

Mr. Weaver and I went to Chincoteague, Virginia, to fish for flounder in the spring. He had a fourteen-foot aluminum boat with a nine-horsepower motor which we towed from Culpeper to the shore. Every time he would catch a fish, his eyes would light up and a big grin would come across his face. One summer, we towed that little boat all the was to Garden City, South Carolina. Another summer, we took the family and towed the boat to Nags Head, North Carolina. One day we maneuvered the boat through a canal to get to the Albemarle Sound. On the way, we hit something solid and put a small hole in the bottom of the boat. We hurried back to shore to get it repaired.

Several days later, we decided to go crabbing. We took the newly repaired boat out again. We crabbed for several hours and caught three crabs, hardly enough to feed our vacationing family of six. He said to me, "We cannot go back with only three crabs!"

I didn't need to ask, "What will we do?" On the way back to our rented house at the beach, we stopped at a store and bought three dozen live crabs to steam. Mrs. Weaver and Maxine thought we had really made a nice catch. We did not tell them the real story until many years later!

Mr. Weaver was a great baseball player at Criglersville High School in Madison County, Virginia. He was a centerfielder who never let a ball pass him. His teammates nicknamed him "Cy," after the famous baseball player Cy Young. He could have received a full scholarship to the University of Virginia to play baseball if his family could have come up with five dollars. Money was very scarce during the Great Depression on the farm. They did not have five dollars. He never regretted that he did not play pro-baseball. He became a self-educated man, doing a lot of reading. In his later years, he became quite a craftsman with wood. We have a beautiful walnut drop-leaf table that he made.

I took over the head football job at Gar-Field and A.T. was head football coach at Fauquier County high School. When our team played them, we beat them. A.T. was not very pleased with his team. Gar-Field went on to tie for the championship in the Battlefield District with James Monroe from Fredericksburg.

In 1964, Woodbridge High School opened taking seventy-five percent of our football players from Gar-Field to their new school. We had a quarterback that season with little talent. He could throw a good pass but did not have good speed, worse yet, he was not the sharpest in making decisions. One time, after a time-out with me on the sidelines, he went to the wrong huddle until the members of the opposing team laughed. The fans probably said, "What a dumb football coach!" That year we won one football game. Needless to say, I got fired as football coach that year and got "kicked upstairs" as assistant principal in charge of discipline. I really hated that job!

In the spring, I had an excellent track member, Melvin Meadows who could do very well in many events in track. I encouraged him to train for the decathlon at a track meet in Northern Virginia. His weakest event was the high hurdles. I always competed against the track members in all field events and in the sprints and hurdles. I felt if they couldn't beat the coach, it would motivate them to do better.

One day I told Melvin, "When you think you can beat me in the high hurdles, let me know. We will have a race." About a week later, he came to track practice and said, "I'm ready to beat you in the high hurdles."

After I got practice organized, I went to Melvin and said, "I am ready to beat you." Prior to that I had a problem with my Achilles tendon in my left foot. I got someone to start us. Most of the track team was watching. Going over the third hurdle, we were tied. As my left foot hit the track, I felt something pop. When I got up, my left foot was sagging with tremendous pain. I told one of the track members to go and get my wife (we lived about one block from the school) to take me to the hospital.

Maxine took me to the Anderson Clinic in Arlington, Virginia. After X-rays, the surgeon came to me and said, "You have severed your Achilles tendon. We will operate tomorrow. By the way, how did you do this? When I told him the story, he said, "How old are you?"

When he heard that I was thirty-four-years-old, he said, "You are a damn fool." I realized that he was right about that!

Surgery was performed the next day and I went home with a cast on my left leg extending from my toes to my hip. I was on crutches and in the cast for three months. Melvin went on and did quite well in the decathlon. In about four weeks, I was scheduled to attend UVA summer school to work on my Master's Degree in Education. What a long summer that was! I had to climb three flights of steps to my room. We did not have an elevator so I had to go up and down those steps for classes.

I felt dejected again when the cast was removed. My calf muscles and thigh muscles had atrophied so much. In fact, my surgeon told me that I would always walk with a limp. After two years of self-therapy, physical and mental, I walked without a limp. Once again Mr. Weaver was my encourager, along with my wife.

The hardest job that I experienced during those years was the assistant principal in charge of discipline. Sam Cox, our principal at Gar-Field High School, was an excellent administrator, a close friend, a good neighbor, a fellow golfer, and a good softball player. The faculty at Gar-Field High School had a slow-pitch softball team in the Fredericksburg League.

When I had to punish a student who had broken a school rule, I could give him an oral reprimand or I could give the student the choice of a suspension from one day up to ten days, or a paddling of three swats. Most of the disobedient kids chose a paddling since missing school would put them behind in their school work. Students were not allowed to make-up the work that they missed. Zeroes were given for the grades missed during suspension time. Most of the parents backed the decisions made by the school. However, if a parent said, "I can't control my child," the administrator had major decisions to make concerning the discipline that was needed. Disruption in the classroom was not allowed!

During this time in 1967, smoking became a terrible habit for me. I was smoking three packs of cigarettes a day. I was constantly being reminded by Maxine and the girls to quit smoking. When we got into the car to go anywhere, the girls and Maxine faked a coughing fit. That didn't help me to decide to quit.

One of the rules for our athletes was "no smoking," yet I smoked in front of them…even during the games. I was a hypocrite! My mother-in-law, Mrs. Weaver, told me she would give me $100 if I would quit. That sounded like a good idea. I talked to Frank Parker and Red Raines, who were also smokers, to join me in quitting. Prior to that, I found it difficult to quit. In fact, I quit everyday but started back the next day. The three of us made an agreement to stop smoking. The one who started back first had to pay the others one-hundred dollars. I was the only one who quit but never got $100!

Mrs. Weaver paid me! She got the money from Mr. Weaver, so I think he played a part in helping me to quit. He had been a former smoker but did quit before my girls were born.

Mr. Weaver, my seventh angel, died in July of 1976 leaving me with one earthly angel, my wife Maxine. In all of the years that I knew him, he helped me in many ways, even lending me money when I needed it. My girls loved him very much and were very sad when he died. Cathie and I sat on his front porch, she in my lap, and we cried together.

Throughout his life, Mr. Weaver mastered every milestone that he encountered. He would have told you that the biggest challenge that he had was trying to teach junior high boys in Sunday School at the Culpeper Baptist Church (nobody else could make them listen or behave).

Mrs. Weaver was still grieving over his death when she died at the age of ninety-one in 2003. I also grieved because I had no Dad. I was left fatherless again.

Chapter Eight

My Heavenly Angel, 1967

After five of my earthly angels died, I tried to be an earthly angel to others. Bo Cardelli, a former football player of mine, was a senior at Gar-Field. In the summer of that year, his father died. He took it very hard. He played football at Gar-Field so he was kept busy during the season. I talked with him quite often and had great empathy for him.

When football season was over, I took Bo as my guest to our hunt club in Richardsville. About a week before we went, I said, "Get a hunting license and a big game stamp to tag a deer before we go."

We left before daybreak and arrived at the hunt club. I stationed him on my favorite stand. A short time later I heard a shot and heard him shout, "I got one!" When I arrived, he had killed an eight-point buck, a nice one. I field-dressed it and asked him for the tag. He said, "I did not have time to get a hunting license." We covered the deer with leaves, drove to Culpeper which was about twenty miles away, and got a tag. We returned to find the deer where we left it. We were lucky no hunter found that deer. We tagged the deer and took it to a check-in station in Richardsville and to a deer-processing place to have it prepared for the freezer. When I asked Bo if he would like to have the head mounted, he excitedly replied, "Yes, sir!" I hope he still has it somewhere as a souvenir.

In May of 1967, our family of four moved from Gar-Field Estates to Featherstone Shores, one block from the Potomac River in Woodbridge, Virginia. Since we lived close to the river, I bought the fourteen-foot aluminum boat and nine-power engine from Mr. Weaver. Maxine, the girls, and I enjoyed riding on the river and especially fishing.

One day in May I invited Bo to go fishing with me. No other boats were docked in the water yet because it was unseasonably cold. We left the shore about three o'clock in the afternoon after school was out. After going downstream about a mile, we anchored in a cove and fished. After catching a few fish and several hours later, I looked across the river and saw white caps. The water was getting really rough. I hurriedly picked up the anchor, started the engine, and headed to the main channel to go home. All of a sudden, I heard a "thud" and the propeller stopped moving the boat. We were moving quickly away from the shore by a strong current. We had sheared a pin on the propeller!

I told Bo, "We need to pull out the oars and row to shore as fast as possible." The faster we rowed, the more we went farther into the middle of the Potomac River.

Bo panicked and said, "I'm going to jump

overboard and swim ashore."

He didn't realize the intensity of the waves. I said, "It is over one-hundred yards to shore. The water is too rough for you to make it." He listened to me and stayed in the little boat.

I said, "We need to be calm and take some action." Not knowing what we would do next, I said, "Help me remove the engine from the boat and place it in the center of the boat." After doing this, he sat on the front seat and I sat on the back seat. By this time, it was quite windy and the waves were about two to three feet high.

It was approaching dark when a helicopter from nearby Quantico Marine Base went directly over our boat. I took off my shirt and waved but apparently the pilot did not see us. As we sat riding out the rough water, I recalled that about ten days before that, several marines from Quantico had drowned in this area during training. I did not remind Bo of that but was sure that he remembered. All we could do was to sit, pray, and hope we would not drown. As I prayed, I felt that someone, perhaps an angel from God, was guiding us in the turbulent water. It was dark at this time so we could not see where we were heading as the current was taking us very fast. While praying, I decided that I would try to become a better Christian if the Lord would see us safely ashore somewhere.

Bo and I did not do much talking, probably because he was praying also. At about nine o'clock that night, I heard waves hitting the shore although we could not see because of darkness. We took the oars out from under the seats and rowed as fast as we could in the direction of the crashing waves. All of a sudden, we felt the boat hit solid ground. We had landed on the opposite side of the Potomac River in Maryland.

We got out of the boat, pulled it ashore, and tried to find out where we were. After climbing up the bank, we saw a light in the far distance. The moon was not out that night but somehow we found our way to that light. It was a guarded area at the powder plant in Indian Head, Maryland.

When we arrived at the guarded gate, I explained who we were and what had happened. We were told, "This has happened several times before." The guard asked, "Do you want to make a phone call?"

I replied, "I would like to call my wife!"

In the meantime, Maxine and the girls were wondering what had happened to us. As the phone rang, she was heading to a neighbor's house to ride in a boat to look for us although it was about ten o'clock. Once again the Lord was looking after us. The river was so rough that they might not have made it. On the phone, Maxine said, "Where are you?"

"On the opposite side and downstream of the Potomac River!"

"Are you and Bo okay?"

"Yes, can you come over to pick us up?"

"I will be over as soon as I can find a neighbor to take care of the children."

After a two-hour drive by car, Maxine arrived at Indian Head, Maryland. We had quite an emotional reunion. I thought that maybe my time had come to

Danny and his mother, Florence Brown Crane

Danny's father, Thomas A. Crane

"Mama" and "Daddy" Brown

"Mama" Brown watches "Daddy" teaching Danny to hammer.

Front row from left to right: Harvey Joe Crane, Danny Crane, Stanley Brown, Estil Brown, Clayton Crane. Second row: Maxine Brown Crane, Mama Brown, baby Sammy Crane, Daddy Brown. Third row: Stuart Crane, Hazel Crane, Florence Hiner, Clyde Hiner, Katherine Jones, Jack Jones, Joe Crane.

Danny with his dogs

Cowboys: Danny, Estil Brown, Stanley Brown

"The boys" — Sunday playmates: Harvey Joe Crane, Irvin Daniel Crane, Herbert Clayton Crane, Estil Herbert Brown, Stanley Eugene Brown

Danny and Coach A.T. Howard

Coach A.T. Howard with captain Danny and alternate captain "Jug" Payne

Coach Joe Friedl and Danny

Danny at Concord College

Danny played the guitar rarely in college. This is one of the few times.

WEST VIRGINIA INTERCOLLEGIATE ATHLETIC CONFERENCE

216 Edgewcod Drive
Beckley, W. Va.
Nov. 16, 1954

Dear Sir:

At the request of Concord College, Athens, W. Va.,--member of the West Virginia Intercollegiate Athletic Conference--I am providing you with some pertinent facts in regards to Daniel Crane, The Concord Express, a candidate for LITTLE ALL-aMERICAN honors.

I would request that you study the figures below to see for yourself of his all-around capabilities. Personally, I have seen him play a number of times. He is a 170-pounder and a great broken field runner.

His four years of gaining 2,833 yards is a "modern" Conference record. The Conference records go back only to 1947.

The accompanying inclosed statistic sheet shows that he is up among the leaders in a lot of department.

Concord's coach, Joe Friedl, has asked that if there is anything you can do to help boost Crane as a Little All-american, you will be honoring a fine boy, who is also a slightly better than "B" average student.

CRANE'S RECORD (year by year)

	G	TD	PAT	Pts	TC	Yds	PA	PC	Yds	PI	Yds	P	Ave.	PR	Yds	KR	Yds
1951...8		4	0	24	65	458	3	1	4	1	3	52	36.7	7	64	11x	212
1952...6		1	0	6	52	345	0	0	0	0	0	7	33.3	1	32	0	0
1953...8		13	3	81	125	1012	0	0	0	4	82	18	30.0	15	308	9	25x
1954...9		17	1	103	167	1018	4	0	0	7	131	17	44.2	18	230	11	267
Total.31		35	4	214	409	2833	7	1	4	12	216	94	37.7	41	634	31	730

Abbreviations: G--games. TD--touchdowns. PAT--points after. Pts--Points. TC--times carried. Yds--Yards rushing. PA--passes attempted. PC--passes completed. Yds--Yds by passing. PI--passes intercepted. Yds--yards returned. P--punts and average. PR--punt returns & yards. KR--Kickoff returns and yards.

The 409 carries for 2,833 yards gives him a 6.9 yard per carry average.

In addition in four years he has caught 24 passes, good for 507 yards and four touchdowns. His total offensive mark, rushing and passing is 2,837.

Adding this 2837 to yards gained passing, returning interceptions, punts and kickoffs, he has a grand OFFENSIVE total of running 4,924 yards. His average pass reception is 21.1 yds; interception return-18.0; punt return-15.4; kickoff return-23.6

Thank you for your attention.

GEORGE SPRINGER, Executive-Secretary

NATIONAL FOOTBALL LEAGUE
STANDARD PLAYERS CONTRACT

BETWEEN

PITTSBURGH STEELERS SPORTS, INCORPORATED   A CORPORATION OF THE STATE OF PENNSYLVANIA.
which operates ..PITTSBURGH STEELERS FOOTBALL CLUB.., and which is a member of the National Football
League, and which is hereinafter called the "Club," and .....DANIEL CRANE........................... of
508 ALBEMARLE STREET, BLUEFIELD, W. VA. hereinafter called the "Player."

In consideration of the respective promises herein the parties hereto agree as follows:

1. The term of this contract shall be from the date of execution hereof until the first day of May following
the close of the football season commencing in ....**1955**............., subject however, to rights of prior
termination as specified herein.

2. The Player agrees that during the term of this contract he will play football and will engage in activities related to football only for the Club and as directed by the Club according to the Constitution, By-Laws,
Rules and Regulations of the National Football League, hereinafter called the "League," and of the Club, and
the Club, subject to the provisions hereof, agrees during such period to employ the Player as a skilled football player. The Player agrees during the term of this contract to report promptly for the Club's training
seasons to render his full time services during the training seasons and at the Club's direction to participate
in all practise sessions and in all League and other football games scheduled by the Club.

3. For the Player's services as a skilled football player during the term of this contract, and for his agreement not to play football or engage in activities related to football for any other person, firm, corporation or institution during the term of this contract, and for the option hereinafter set forth giving the Club the right to
renew this contract, and for the other undertakings of the Player herein, the Club promises to pay the Player
each football season during the term of this contract the sum of $..**4,500.00**...... to be payable as follows:
     **75% of said salary in weekly installments commencing with the first and ending with the last regularly
     scheduled League game played by the Club during such season and the balance of 25% of said sum at
     the end of said last regularly scheduled League game.**
In addition, the Club promises and agrees to pay the reasonable board and lodging expenses of the Player in-
curred while playing games for the Club in other than the Club's home city and also to pay all proper and
necessary travelling expenses of the Player and his meals en route to and from said games.

4. The Player agrees at all times to comply with and to be bound by all the provisions of the Constitution,
By-Laws, Rules and Regulations of the League and of the Club, all of which are hereby made a part of this
contract. If the Player fails to comply with said Constitution, By-Laws, Rules and Regulations the Club shall
have the right to terminate this contract or to take such other action as may be specified in said Constitution,
By-laws, Rules and Regulations, or as may be directed by the Commissioner of the League, hereinafter called the
"Commissioner." The Player agrees to submit himself to the discipline of the League and of the Club for any
violation of such Constitution, By-laws, Rules and Regulations subject however, to the right to a hearing by the
Commissioner. All matters in dispute between the Player and the Club shall be referred to the Commissioner
and his decision shall be accepted as final, complete, conclusive, binding and unappealable, by the Player and
by the Club. The Player hereby waives any and all rights of action against the Commissioner, the League, the
Club or any of its members or stockholders, and against any officer of the Club or of the League arising out of
or in connection with decisions of the Commissioner, except to the extent of awards made by the Commissioner
to the Player. The Player hereby acknowledges that he has read said Constitution, By-Laws, Rules and Regulations and that he understands their meaning.

5. The Player promises and agrees that during the term of this contract he will not play football or engage
in activities related to football for any other person, firm, corporation or institution except with the prior written
consent of the Club and the Commissioner, and that he will not during the term of this contract engage in any
game or exhibition of baseball, basketball, hockey, wrestling boxing or any other sport which endangers his
ability to perform his services hereunder, without the prior written consent of the Club. The Player likewise
promises and agrees that during the term of this contract, when, as and if he shall receive an invitation to participate in any All-Star football game which is approved by the League, he will play in said game in accordance
with all the terms and conditions relating thereto, including the player compensation therein set forth, as are
agreed to between the League and the Sponsor of such game.

6. The Player represents and warrants that he is and will continue to be sufficiently highly skilled in all
types of football team play to play professional football of the caliber required by the League and by the Club,
that he is and will continue to be in excellent physical condition, and agrees to perform his services hereunder
to the complete satisfaction of the Club and its Head Coach. If in the opinion of the Head Coach the Player does
not maintain himself in excellent physical condition or fails at any time during the football seasons included in
the term of this contract to demonstrate sufficient skill and capacity to play professional football of the caliber
required by the League and by the Club, or if in the opinion of the Head Coach the Player's work or conduct
in the performance of this contract is unsatisfactory as compared with the work and conduct of other members
of the Club's squad of players, the Club shall have the right to terminate this contract upon written notice to the
player of such termination.

7. Upon termination of this contract the Club shall pay the Player only the balance remaining due him for
travelling and board and lodging expenses and any balance remaining due him for football seasons completed
prior to termination, and, if termination takes place during a football season, any balance remaining due him
on that portion of his total compensation for that season as provided in paragraph 3 hereof which the number
of regularly scheduled League games already played by the Club during that season bears to the total number
of League games scheduled for the Club for that season.

8. The Player hereby represents that he has special, exceptional and unique knowledge, skill and ability
as a football player, the loss of which cannot be estimated with any certainty and cannot be fairly or adequately
compensated by damages and therefore agrees that the Club shall have the right, in addition to any other rights
which the Club may possess, to enjoin him by appropriate injunction proceedings against playing football or en-
gaging in activities related to football for any person, firm, corporation or institution and against any other breach
of this contract.

1956 All Army Football team in Germany

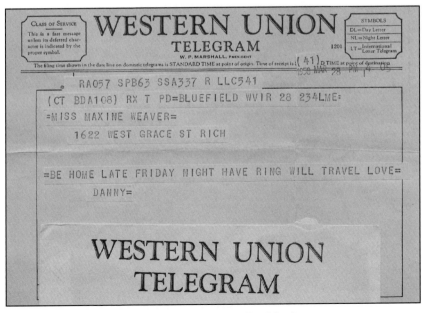

Danny's clever proposal to Maxine

From left to right: Margaret Ellen Quaintance, Nancy Eyerly, Pat Perry, Patricia Hayes, Wyvonne Weaver Vance, Maxine Weaver, Charles Elton Weaver, Pansy Frazier Weaver, Vanessa Vance, and Florence Crane Hiner.

Maxine and Danny Crane - August 9, 1958

Coach Danny at Gar-Field High School

(Left) Danny coaches a muddy game with Spotsylvania High School.

(Below) Danny with track team members

FOOTBALL

Verlin "Sparky" Adams, Morris Harvey
Norman Allison, Fairmont State
Pete Anania, Morris Harvey
Tony Anastasio, West Liberty State
Emory Anderson, Davis & Elkins
William Anderson, West Liberty State

Forrest Bechtel, W. Va. Wesleyan
Daniel Bailey, Concord
James Bailey, West Virginia State
Neal Balal, West Virginia Tech
Leonard "Fente" Barnett, W. Va. Wesleyan
William Basham, Concord
Cliff "Gryp" Battles, W. Va. Wesleyan
Charles Baxter, Concord
John Beane, West Virginia Tech
Howard Bechtold, West Liberty State
Don Bennett, Fairmont State
Paul Billard, West Liberty State
Ed Billingham, Fairmont State
Cosby Blackwood, Morris Harvey
Allen Blair, West Liberty State
Gary Blake, Glenville State
Al Blumih, West Liberty State
Tom Blandin, W. Va. Wesleyan
Lovie Bohince, Salem
John Solee, Bluefield State
Sante Boninsegna, Concord
Tom Bossie, Morris Harvey
Sam Bouche, Concord
Sam Bowers, Concord
Preston Bowes, Concord
Meredith Boyd, Shepherd
Bill Brown, Concord
Richard Brown, West Liberty State
Roy Brown, Morris Harvey
Carl Brummage, Davis & Elkins
Ellsworth Buck, Glenville State
Steve Burda, West Liberty State
Robert Burkhart, Salem
Ron Burkhart, Salem
Harry Burner, Fairmont State
Woodrow Burton, W. Va. Wesleyan
Dick Busby, West Liberty State

Bob Campiglio, West Liberty State
James Carey, Shepherd
Burwell "Jim" Carey, West Liberty State
Glynn Carlock, Concord
Kent Carpenter, W. Va. Wesleyan
Jimmy Carr, Morris Harvey
Virgil Carr, Morris Harvey
Jim Cherelcol, Fairmont State
John Chrobis, Glenville State
Phil Clarks, Glenville State
George Clayton, Fairmont State
Hank Cleary, Fairmont State
Clifford Clem, Salem
Jerry Colan, W. Va. Wesleyan
Harry Colabrese, Salem
Billy Connors, Salem
Randy Cooper, West Virginia Tech
Lester Corzine, Davis & Elkins
James Coulter, West Liberty State
Dan Crane, Concord
Tom Cuppett, Salem
Frank Curtis, Davis & Elkins
Dusan Cvkic, Concord
Lewis D'Antom, Concord
Ed Davidek, West Liberty State
Jack Davis, West Virginia Tech
Clem Dawson, Fairmont State
Ray DeCola, West Liberty State
Dick Dei, West Liberty State
Don DeLongo, West Liberty State
Tony DeMatteo, Davis & Elkins
Patsy DiPompaolo, West Liberty State
Nick Di Pietro, W. Va. Wesleyan
Delmar Dixon, West Virginia Tech
Andy Donaldzeizh, Morris Harvey
Charles "Chuck" Donley, W. Va. Wesleyan
Charles Donnelly, W. Va. Wesleyan
Jack Dameron, West Liberty State
Don Doran, Fairmont State
Boyd Dotson, W. Va. Wesleyan
James Dotson, Glenville State
Clyde Downs, Morris Harvey
Dennis Drenning, W. Va. Wesleyan
Mike Durbin, Concord
Jim Dyer, Morris Harvey

Dick Edge, West Liberty State
Orville Edmondson, W. Va. Wesleyan
Norman Edwards, West Virginia Tech
Gordon Eleason, Glenville State
Darrell Elam, West Virginia Tech
William Elias, Salem
Harold Erwin, Glenville State
Wayne Everly, Shepherd
Bill Ewuslak, Fairmont State

Martin Fagter, Salem
Phillip "Butch" Farley, Concord
Robert Farmer, Concord
Robert Fair, W. Va. Wesleyan
James Fazzioto, Shepherd
John "Ace" Federovitch, Davis & Elkins
Bob Felty, Morris Harvey
Ben Fluharty, Davis & Elkins
Carl Fodor, West Liberty State
Alan Frazee, Fairmont State
Eugene Fritte, West Virginia Tech
Albert "Butzy" Fultz, Fairmont State

John Garrett, Salem
Bill Garten, Concord
Ronald Gaudi, Salem
Nick Giantonio, W. Va. Wesleyan
John Gilmore, West Virginia State
Dick Glover, West Liberty State
Darrell Goff, Glenville State
Charles Goodman, West Virginia Tech
Loren Green, Salem
William Gregory, Davis & Elkins
Moses Gyln, Fairmont State
Tom Gunnoe, Glenville State
Sinfon Gurneau, Davis & Elkins
Gene Gurtis, Morris Harvey
Ed Gutowski, Davis & Elkins

Ray Hadd, Broaddus
William Hahn, Shepherd
Richard Haines, West Liberty State
David Hale, W. Va. Wesleyan
Ken Hamilton, West Liberty State
Bill Hanlin, Glenville State
Norman Harlan, West Virginia Tech
Dick Harmleson, Shepherd
Kenneth Harris, West Liberty State
Richard Harris, Fairmont State
Richard Hart, Shepherd
Harry Hartman, Salem
James Hawkins, W. Va. Wesleyan
Albert Hawley, Davis & Elkins
Bill Heyburtsl, Fairmont State
William Hedrick, Concord
Dana Hemrock, West Liberty State
Ed Helminski, Fairmont State
Wayne Hicks, Concord
Hubert Hinchman, West Virginia Tech
Glenn Hiser, W. Va. Wesleyan
Joe Hockman, Shepherd
Joe Hofzeiher, Concord
Burzi Holmes, West Liberty State
Robert Holstein, West Virginia State
John Hoover, Glenville State
George Holt, Shepherd
Dale Hounshell, Fairmont State
Clyde "Bud" Hutson, Davis & Elkins

Bob Irwin, Davis & Elkins
Cecil Irwin, Davis & Elkins

Roy Jackson, Fairmont State
John Janicki, Fairmont State
Jack Johnson, W. Va. Wesleyan
Arthur Jones, W. Va. Wesleyan
Cornelius Jones, West Virginia State
Cliff Judy, W. Va. Wesleyan

Maurice Kalin, Fairmont State
Marvin Kapp, Davis & Elkins
Bill Karpinionis, Glenville State
Tom Karlo, Concord
Clark Keene, West Virginia Tech
Earl Keener, Fairmont State
Ed Kelly, Morris Harvey
Ray Kelly, Davis & Elkins
J. D. Kidd, Morris Harvey
William King, Concord
Bill Kinzer, Glenville State
Sam Kistler, Salem
David Knight, Fairmont State
Louis Kolopous, W. Va. Wesleyan
Eddie Koaks, W. Va. Wesleyan
Frank Kovach, Morris Harvey

Paul Krymenacker, Salem
Ed Kuchar, Davis & Elkins
William Rugler, Salem
Mike Kurka, West Liberty State
Bob Kusserow, West Liberty State

Jack Labay, W. Va. Wesleyan
Dick Laughlin, Fairmont State
James Laughlin, Glenville State
Ralph Lehman, Shepherd
Tonna Lewis, West Virginia Tech
Tom Lewis, Fairmont State
Jim Lipinski, Fairmont State
Steve Lipscomb, Fairmont State
Jim Lockhart, West Virginia Tech
George Lohman, W. Va. Wesleyan
Clarence "Pug" Lowery, Morris Harvey

Homer Maddox, Shepherd
Hugh Manley, West Liberty State
Sam Marchio, Glenville State
John Maria, Glenville State
Earl Marshall, West Liberty State
Cecil Mason, Fairmont State
Ralph Mattison, Davis & Elkins
John Mazzie, W. Va. Wesleyan
Tom McCort, Salem
Leon McCoy, Morris Harvey
Don McDowell, Bluefield State
Fred McGlothlin, West Virginia State
Randall "Rand" McKinney, Davis & Elkins
Addison McKown, W. Va. Wesleyan
Paul McKoem, Glenville State
Jim McMillion, Glenville State
Steve McMillion, Glenville State
William McShane, West Liberty State
Don Merriman, Glenville State
Jim Miles, Concord
Aaron Miller, Fairmont State
Joe Miller, Morris Harvey
Leo Miller, West Liberty State
Parker "Pat" Mistretta, W. Va. Wesleyan
Frank Montrose, Glenville State
John Moore, W. Va. Wesleyan
Kenneth Moore, W. Va. Wesleyan
Nick Moreman, Fairmont State
Alton Morford, Glenville State
Archie Morris, Glenville State
John Mowry, Glenville State
Gary Moyer, Fairmont State
Tom Muhsey, Concord
George Murphy, Fairmont State
Gerald Myers, West Liberty State

Robert Nebel, West Liberty State

Wendell O'Dell, Glenville State
Gene Oglesby, West Virginia Tech

Tom Pannett, West Liberty State
Bill Parry, West Liberty State
Russell "Russ" Parsons, West Virginia Tech
Everett Pearcy, Salem
Pete Perri, Salem
Nelson Peterson, W. Va. Wesleyan
Al Phillips, Davis & Elkins
Bruce Phillips, Shepherd
George Phillips, Concord
John Pike, Davis & Elkins
John Posadia, Glenville State
Donald Pitts, Bluefield State
Russell "Tootie" Porterfield, Glenville State
Harrold Porterfield, Glenville State
Vinson Post, Glenville State
Ray Prentti, West Liberty State
Keith Pritt, Glenville State
Ray Pullen, W. Va. Wesleyan
Robert Pulice, West Virginia Tech

John Quintrell, Glenville State

Alex Radoo, West Virginia Tech
Walter Raspko, West Virginia Tech
Carlos Ratliff, Glenville State
Dave Reensnyder, W. Va. Wesleyan
Paul Reger, West Liberty State
Robert Reiber, Fairmont State
Neil Rengle, Davis & Elkins
Gordon Rennie, Fairmont State
Louie Ribel, Fairmont State
Jesse Rodriguez, Salem
Kelly Rodriguez, W. Va. Wesleyan
Tom Rogers, Glenville State
Oswald Romato, West Liberty State
Dewey Romine, Morris Harvey
Bill Roney, Concord

Alex Roscoe, West Liberty State
Francis Rycroaky, West Liberty State

Harry Seltzer, Morris Harvey
Denver Sayre, West Liberty State
Dave Schaffner, W. Va. Wesleyan
Earl Schaub, West Liberty State
Robert Scheurz, West Liberty State
Wilbur Scott, West Liberty State
Harden "Whitey" Scragg, Morris Harvey
John Shearer, Shepherd
Harry "Bud" Shelton, Davis & Elkins
Dale Shenal, Salem
Charles Shophard, W. Va. Wesleyan
Bill Shinn, Glenville State
Francis Simena, Concord
Doug Simmons, West Virginia Tech
Jack Sims, West Virginia Tech
Watoon Skinner, Fairmont State
Pete Smitzer, Concord
Keith Smith, Glenville State
Zygmunde "Ziggy" Sobek, Salem
Gene Spadaro, Glenville State
Ancil Sparks, Concord
Harry Spears, W. Va. Wesleyan
Ben Specs, West Liberty State
Oscar Speiser, West Liberty State
Marion Spelock, West Virginia Tech
Charles Spencer, Glenville State
Bob Spenik, Morris Harvey
Larry "Bill" Stanley, Glenville State
Robert "Babe" Starrett, Morris Harvey
Doug Stone, Salem
Robert Straight, W. Va. Wesleyan
Dick Sturm, Salem
Clyde Sweeney, Salem
Forrest Swisher, Salem
Leland Swor, West Virginia Tech

Kenneth Talbott, Davis & Elkins
John Talts, Fairmont State
Sam Taylor, Shepherd
Arl Tabor, Davis & Elkins
Ed Talaeli, Glenville State
Jack Tennant, Glenville State
Darrell Tenney, W. Va. Wesleyan
Clarence "Bud" Tesch, Salem
John Thacker, Morris Harvey
Robert Tolley, West Virginia Tech
Gerald Townson, West Virginia Tech
Miles Trout, Morris Harvey
Pete Tuccio, West Liberty State
Guy Tucker, Shepherd

Forrest "Spike" Underwood, Davis & Elkins

Harry Vernon, Salem
Gerald Vaugh, Morris Harvey
Frank Vincent, Glenville State
Foster Vittone, Morris Harvey

Ted Warobiak, W. Va. Wesleyan
Claude Warren, Davis & Elkins
Ray Watson, Glenville State
Claude Watts, Bluefield State
Blair Wenge, West Virginia Tech
David Wergano, Salem
Dale Wells, West Virginia Tech
Colton Welsh, Morris Harvey
Elton Whanger, Concord
Charles White, W. Va. Wesleyan
Robert White, W. Va. Wesleyan
John Whitfield, Davis & Elkins
Newton Whittaker, Salem
Don Widdjoav, Shepherd
Don Williams, Concord
Walter Willson, West Liberty State
Emmett Wilson, Glenville State
W. R. "Squibb" Wilson, Fairmont State
Jackson Witt, West Liberty State
Darwin Wolfe, Fairmont State
Bill Wood, W. Va. Wesleyan

Don Yantis, Concord
Bill Young, West Liberty State
Robert "Froggy" Young, West Virginia Tech

Jim Youngblood, Fairmont State

Leo Zille, West Liberty State
Zigmund Zimoski, Salem
Sam Zinrich, W. Va. Wesleyan

D. Banks Wilburn
WVIAC President

George Springer
WVIAC Commissioner

A.T. Howard with Cheryl Crane and Cathie Crane

Danny graduated from the University of Virginia with a Master's Degree in Secondary Education.

Hall of Fame at Concord College

Cathie and Lucky 7 graduated from Averett College in 1984.

Jim Knepp, Maxine, and Danny are practicing for a performance with the Circuit Riding Singers in Culpeper, Virginia.

The Circuit Riding Singers are from left to right: "Red" Jenkins, Marge Arnold, Emily Bussenger, Jim Knepp, Louise Batten, Clarence Batten, Robert Aylor, and Dan Arnold. Not pictured are Mary Ann Knepp, Charlie Bussenger, and Naomi Aylor.

This is the retired jersey that was framed. Later, the jersey was "lost." Notice the name!

Maxine and Danny celebrating 50 years - "my #1 angel"

This is a scene from Graves Mountain Lodge in Syria, Virginia.

At the farm in Madison, Virginia, Danny is teaching grandson Seth Chain to hit the bull's eye.

Cousin Allen Crane and Danny won the Member/Guest Golf Tournament in 1994 at the Fauquier Springs Country Club in Warrenton, Virginia.

It is almost impossible to get a photo of the family, but Danny gathered them all together at Christmas in 2003. From left to right on the back row: Daniel Reel, Seth Chain, Aaron Reel, Cathie Reel, Bill Reel, and from left to right on the front row: Cheryl Crane and Maxine. Today the family has enlarged to where it is impossible to get them all into one picture!

Steven Ray Chain was the first great-grandson. He was born August 24, 2006. Pictured are his mother Jessica, his grandmother Cheryl, his father Seth, and baby Steven.

Grandson Daniel Reel married November 13, 2010. Pictured from left to right are Danny; Aaron Reel; Maxine; Lauren and Daniel Reel; Cathie and Bill Reel.

Steven and Cheyenne Chain celebrated Easter of 2012 at Danny and Maxine's home in North Carolina. "Sissy" was born March 3, 2009.

Danny's sisters: Joan Hiner Groves and Peggy Hiner Moynahan.

Danny goes back to LaGrange as often as he can. The farmhouse where he was born in now owned by Margie and Estil Brown.

On any given day, Danny can be found fishing from his back yard.

meet the Lord. We left the boat there and went back several days later to tow it back home. We repaired the pin and had the boat back in the water several days later. Bo and I remained friends for several years after that experience.

Shortly after this experience, I decided to rededicate my life to the Lord. I decided to become a Baptist after being raised a Methodist. Maxine was still a member in the Culpeper Baptist Church and I was still a member in the Hopewell Methodist Church. Since we could not decide which one would change memberships, we alternated going to different churches. I needed to change and our girls needed Sunday School training. We joined Calvary Baptist Church in Gar-Field Estates.

Meeting with the deacons, I was told that I did not have to be baptized again to join the church. Since I was rededicating my life to the Lord, I decided to be baptized by immersion. After that I became a Sunday School teacher for the youth.

Chapter Nine

Transitions, 1970-1980's

After three years as assistant principal at Gar-Field High School, I wanted to return to coaching football and track. I talked to Bill Holsclaw, head football coach at Osbourn High School in Manassas. He and I had been rivals in the early sixties, since there were only two high schools in Prince William County. He wanted me to be his backfield coach in football and he would be my assistant track coach in the spring. I was hired to those responsibilities as well as being a physical science teacher. For several years, we had great experiences and still remain friends today.

About this time, I received word from Concord College that my retired jersey, number 28, had been stolen in the transfer from the old gym to the new gym. Ira Blankenship was athletic director and he did not notify me of what had happened. No one ever found the jersey.

Also, at that time, I was mailed my football NAIA All-American ring which had been in a desk drawer at Concord since 1955. My dedication to Concord was tarnished. I could not understand why those things were happening. I decided not to pursue any of that since I was quite busy in my coaching, teaching, and child rearing.

In 1972, I became assistant principal at Stonewall Jackson High School. Bill Wood, a former rival football coach, was instrumental in getting me that job. Our families became very close. Sometimes I jogged over to his house, which was about a half-mile away, and asked his wife Emily to give me a snack.

Bill and I were golfers together. He was quite good. We always walked and carried our bags. One day we were playing at Greenwich Golf Course about three miles from Manassas. On hole number three, when I got to the green, I became very dizzy. I lay down on the green and felt like it was spinning around. I had cramps in my hands and had pains and a tightness in my chest. Bill wanted to go for help, but I said, "I'll be all right in a minute."

"I'll go get a golf cart at the club house," he said.

"I can walk back." I did walk back to the club house and Bill carried my golf bag, the longest walk I have ever had!

After several hours at Prince William County Hospital, it was diagnosed that I had angina, a heart condition. At the age of thirty-nine, I was devastated that I had heart trouble. I became withdrawn and waited to die at any moment. The heart specialist prescribed nitroglycerin to take in case I had an attack of angina. I detested taking it since it gave me a severe headache.

After several months, with the help from an angel of the Lord, I decided to go on with my life as if no health problem existed.

My family and I joined the Manassas Baptist Church and became quite active there. Our two girls, Cathie and Cheryl, became active in the youth group. Maxine sang in the choir and I became a deacon for the first time. Our family made many Christian friends in that church.

In 1974 I went to Woodbridge High School as a biology teacher and head track coach for indoor and outdoor track. The job was offered to me by principal Hugh Browning and athletic director, Butch Farley. While there, I discovered that the athletes at Woodbridge were men, not boys, in stature. The football team played Bethel High School from Virginia Beach for the state championship and lost by a close score. The stadium had been named the "A.T. Howard Memorial Stadium" several years after Coach Howard died. I helped the head football coach call plays from the upstairs press box.

On November 15, 1974, Maxine and I flew to Parkersburg, West Virginia, where I was inducted into the West Virginia Intercollegiate Athletic Conference All-Time; All- Conference Squad for football. It was composed of the selection of the best football players for fifty years in the WVIAC, from 1924-1974. I met many of the players face to face that I had played football against. I was selected to give a short speech for the group of players from 1951-1954. The football coach who had been at Shepherd was there but did not have too many words with me. It was one of the best honors that I have ever received. Thanks to my earthly angel, Coach Friedl, who nominated me. There were fifteen colleges involved and only one-hundred-eleven players were selected out of fourteen-thousand players.

When our daughter Cheryl was at Osbourn High School, in Manassas, she went out for the track team. She had the potential for being good in jumping events and in sprints. She was very fast and well-coordinated. One day during practice, she fell while running because her ankle locked on her. She was not injured seriously but she decided not to stay with track. I told her, "If you don't enjoy it, don't run track." She gave it up and became a very good cheerleader.

Cheryl also believes in earthly angels since she hides one in every painting that she does. She has many illustrations in the book *Ask for Nothing* that my wife wrote. Cheryl was schooled at the Art Institute of Atlanta and the Art Academy of Cincinnati. She also has a Master's Degree from Virginia Commonwealth University. At the time of this writing, she teaches art at Brooke Point High School in Stafford, Virginia.

Winter track found us taking long trips to Lynchburg, Williamsburg, the Naval Academy, and other places to participate in meets. We had no indoor track at Woodbridge, so we ran the halls during cold weather and practiced outside on the asphalt track when it was warm enough. At that time, Woodbridge was on shifts because of over-crowdedness. I taught five classes of biology a day and had three track practices: one for the morning shift, one for the overlapping shift, and one for the afternoon shift. I was living in Manassas and commuting to Woodbridge, about a thirty-minute drive. I left home at six o'clock in the morning since my first class was at seven o'clock. My last practice was over at five-thirty, so my day began at six in the morning and ended at seven at night. The winter track program was quite successful.

On the way back from an indoor track meet at Lynchburg College on a Wednesday night at approximately ten-thirty, our school bus broke down. School was scheduled for the next day and the weather forecast was for snow to begin early the next morning. We were located about fifteen miles south of Lovingston. No cell phones were invented yet so we had no method of communication to seek help. There was a house on a hill to the right of us which had a light burning. I went and knocked on the door. A Negro gentleman answered the door. I said, "We are a track team from Woodbridge on our way from an indoor track meet at Lynchburg College. Our bus has broken down so we need to call for help."

He said, "I'm sorry you have a problem, but I can't help. I don't have a telephone." I was so dejected. I walked back to the bus.

About forty-five minutes passed without any traffic. The track members were getting cold. Suddenly, we saw the lights from a pick-up truck traveling south toward Lynchburg. The gentleman heading to work at a power plant. He stopped and asked us about our problem. The bus driver explained what had happened. The engineer looked under the hood of the bus and immediately saw the problem. He said, "I don't have the part needed to repair the engine, but I think I can try to rig a part to last until you get home."

After what seemed like an hour, he said to the bus driver, "Try to start the engine." After the second try, the engine started!

We were a bunch of "happy campers." I told the engineer, "You are a heavenly angel sent by God to help us with this crisis." I shook his hand and offered to pay him for his time. He refused. I thanked him and told him goodbye.

We arrived back at Woodbridge several hours later. After waiting for all of the parents to pick-up their children, I took my thirty-minute drive to Manassas. The snow did not materialize, and I had a seven o'clock class the next morning. I probably got about three hours of sleep that night.

Outdoor track began on a high note. The talented athletes worked very hard. We went to the Harrington Relays at Washington and Lee High School in Arlington, Virginia, and won the meet. It was the first time that Edison High School did not win that meet in several years. Coach Cook was very upset that his team did not win. Our athletes were very proud to bring home the trophy from that prestigious meet.

We went back to practice and won many track meets that year. In the state track meet at the University of Virginia, we placed third in the meet with the majority of our athletes returning for the next year. Maxine met us at that meet and while we stood there talking, Coach Sonny Randle, head football coach at UVA came up to talk to us. I had played football with Sonny at CCHS before he went to Fork Union Military Academy. Maxine had dated him while he was at FUMA and had been given a football letter on a sweater from him. Sonny had played pro-football with the St. Louis Cardinals for several years.

One of the first things Maxine said to Sonny was, "What are you doing these days?" You should have seen his reaction!

Sonny said, "I am head football coach at the University of Virginia!" Not having anymore conversation with her, he bade farewell and we haven't seen him since.

After placing third in the State Meet that year and with most of the talented athletes returning, we were the favorite team to win the State Track Meet the following year.

In the spring of 1975, Maxine and I flew to Charleston, West Virginia, where I was inducted into the fifty-years All-Time; All-Conference Track Team from 1924-1974. Although we did not have a track team at Concord in 1951-1955, Coach Bo Baxter had nominated me. I had participated in the Southern Conference Track Meet at the University of North Carolina in Chapel Hill, and twice at the WVIAC state meet in Bethany, West Virginia.

I wanted to acknowledge Bo Baxter for all that he had done for me. I asked him if I could nominate him to the Hall of Fame at Concord, but he refused saying that it would not be fair for him to be selected since many who deserved it had not been selected.

In 1975, indoor track or winter track at Woodbridge High School was very difficult since we had lots of snow and cold weather. We did take some long trips and won several meets. The teams around us did not beat us, and we had several individual champions in large meets. One of the most outstanding individuals was Russell Davis who high jumped six-feet-nine-inches, long jumped, and ran sprints. After graduation, he went to the University of Michigan on a football scholarship and played football for the Pittsburg Steelers.

Jimmy Little, a hurdler, broke several school records and had a football scholarship to Arizona State University. Harold Anderson was a sprinter who broke several records by running the one-hundred-dash in less than ten seconds. He did not have the ability to play college football and not enough talent to run track in college. Our winter track team had a great year. We were looking forward to winning the state outdoor track meet since we had broken twenty-two records in track in a year-and-a-half. What a talented track team! I could hardly wait for the spring track to begin. My assistant track coach and head cross country coach, Jim Rogers, was excellent in coaching middle distance and long distance runners.

When spring came in 1976, Jim and I were preparing for a state championship trophy in track. Most of the track athletes from the previous year had returned. We had so much talent. In April, our team was invited to participate in the William and Mary track meet in Williamsburg, Virginia, to participate in the high school division. There was also a college division.

Many schools and colleges from the east coast were invited to this large meet.

Our track team performed really well with our individual champions and we won the high school division. As Jim and I were leaving the stadium, we saw four athletes with cans of beer in their hands...our track members! I had a policy of "no smoking" and "no drinking of alcoholic beverages" while in training. After confronting them, I told them to turn in their uniforms when we got back to school. They were still wearing their green and gold Woodbridge sweats. I cringed when I thought what the other teams thought about Woodbridge High School. It was a quiet ride from Williamsburg to Woodbridge that day. With the decision that I had made, we had no chance at winning the Triple-A State Track Meet.

When we arrived back at school, I collected the uniforms from the four athletes and wished them luck. I called our principal, Hugh Browning, and explained the situation to him. He reassured me that he would back me on the position I had taken. Next, I called the parents of the four athletes and explained what I had seen and the action that I had taken. They were shocked at what had happened and did not like my decision. Later, I found out that the main thing they were concerned about was, "Will Coach Crane inform the college or university at which our sons have football scholarships?" (I did not.)

As the season progressed, our team did have a winning season, but did not win the state track meet. I was so devastated that I decided not to be a head coach anymore, perhaps not to coach anymore. At the end of the season, I had a meeting with the track team and told them that I was resigning as track coach and moving to another school. I had already notified Coach Rogers and recommended him to become the head track coach at Woodbridge High School for the next year. Saying goodbye to that team was one of the hardest things that I have ever done, I even cried while talking to them.

In the fall of 1976, I transferred to Stonewall Jackson High School in Manassas. There I worked closely with Emily and Bill Wood. Bill was in the Guidance Department and helped me to get outstanding students in biology. There I had some of the most outstanding students and best-behaved students that I have ever taught. I thought that I had died and gone to heaven! In addition, I was assistant track coach in indoor and outdoor track. We did not have an indoor track, but had wonderful facilities for biology lectures and many lab areas. Although we had some individual champions, our track teams at Stonewall Jackson did not win any large meets

During this time, my sixth earthly angel Coach Friedl was still looking out for me. He nominated me to the Board of Trustees at Concord College, and I was selected. After serving on that board for two years, I found it very difficult to travel from Manassas to Athens, West Virginia, for the meetings, so I resigned.

In December of 1977, Maxine's niece Vanessa was getting married to Buzzy Moncure in the Culpeper Baptist Church. I was preparing to go to the wedding when I experienced such pains in my chest that I went

99

to the Culpeper Memorial Hospital. After spending several days in the hospital, I was discharged with "a rheumatoid heart." Looking back at that, I believe it was a misdiagnosis. The doctor on call that night was my mother's doctor in the 1950's. My mother died of rheumatoid arthritis and he assumed I had the same problem. I was released from the hospital without any medication or follow-up of the heart condition.

During the late seventies, my younger daughter, Cathie, and I were training her horse, Lucky, to compete in a horse show. She got Lucky for Christmas when she was ten-years-old and Lucky was a young, untrained quarter-horse. He was boarded on a nearby farm in Manassas. I did not know much about training a horse, although I had been around them on our farm at LaGrange. Cathie knew how to lead the horse in circles since she had taken riding lessons.

Day after day, we led Lucky around the paddock. Our next procedure for training was to put a saddle on Lucky and lead him around until he got used to the saddle. Next, I put Cathie on the saddle. At that point in our training, we did not allow Lucky to walk with Cathie on his back. After that, I led Lucky in a circle around the paddock with Cathie in the saddle.

The day finally came when I was sure that Lucky was ready to be ridden! As a part of our board, we had to feed Lucky every day. One day Cathie was sick and could not go to feed, so I went by myself. I did not take time to put a saddle on, I got on Lucky's back. Guess what! He bucked and threw me off. Luckily I was not hurt, so I got back on him and he obeyed me.

I didn't tell Cathie until many months later! The rest is history…after Cathie groomed him and trained him, Maxine and I took Cathie to many horse shows where she won lots of ribbons.

Maxine is another story with Lucky. She was afraid of the huge animal. Once at a horse show Cathie said, "Mom, hold Lucky's reins for me while I go to get something to drink." She was always too nervous to eat during a horse show.

"You've got to be kidding," she replied. "You know I can't do that!"

"Dad's not around and you've got to do it for me."

Maxine got into the car, rolled down the window, put her hand out the window and said, "Okay, hand me the reins." She held Lucky by the reins (her arm out of the car window) until Cathie returned.

In 1980, Cathie graduated from Osbourn Park High School. She had been accepted to Averett College in Danville, Virginia, to major in equestrian studies. That summer, while riding and jumping in an open field, Lucky got tired of jumping hay bales. She loved jumping and she decided to make him jump "one more jump before I quit." Lucky jumped, but bucked so much that Cathie was thrown from the horse. She lay on the ground and worked her legs continually. Her back hurt, but she called for me to come to get her.

I hurriedly went to the farm and cautiously put her into our brown Ford pickup truck. The bumpy ride was hard on her. I was driving as fast as I could and she was constantly asking, "Can't you slow down a bit?"

After X-rays in the hospital, it was determined that nothing was broken. We helped her to get into our car and headed for home. It was quite a task to get her organized comfortably in her bed. She had excruciating pain in her back. To this day, she can remember that Maxine had fried pork chops, mashed potatoes, and peas for dinner. She was starving and was beginning to eat when the phone rang.

Maxine answered. A doctor from the hospital said, "Get her back to the hospital as soon as you can. She has a fractured vertebrae in the lower part of her back."

Maxine said, "Shall we bring her back in the car or call an ambulance?"

He said, "You've driven her all over the place, you might as well drive her back."

Poor Cathie, she had planned to take her horse to college with her. She was so disappointed. When she went to Averett in the fall, she took only classroom studies for one semester. She began riding again in the fall of 1981, She participated in intercollegiate competition in 1982 and did quite well. In the fall of 1983, Lucky finally got to go to college. They graduated together in 1984.

Chapter Ten

Moving to Culpeper in the 1980's

While Maxine was teaching English at Osbourn Park High School and I was teaching biology and coaching track at Stonewall Jackson High School in Manassas, we were kept quite busy. During that time, we were offering assistance to Mrs. Weaver in Culpeper by helping her to clean, helping her to cook, continuing the gardening that Mr. Weaver always had, trimming the hedge that was on two sides of the property, and mowing the grass. We went to her house every weekend.

Also, we were still keeping the 126 acre farm in Madison from falling apart. (After Mr. Weaver died, the farm was surveyed again and they lost twenty-four acres.) We kept up the fences, mowed the lawn, painted the house inside and outside, and kept control of the ground hogs, etc. We spent our summers at the farm doing work. Cathie loved going to the farm, in fact, she celebrated her birthday every year in October by taking her friends along. Cheryl didn't enjoy the farm as much.

In 1983, one of my earthly angels, Coach Friedl,

died. I did not find out about his death until long after the funeral. He had been like a father to me, not only at Concord but also long after I graduated from college.

In the early 1980's, Frank and Bob Parker and Floyd Foley organized a "Killer Kyle" golf tournament in Northern Virginia for Concord alumni. Frank had been my roommate at Concord and had helped to treat "Charlie horses" and other injuries so I could play football the following week. Later, while in graduate school with him at UVA, he encouraged me when I got depressed to keep on studying and not go home.

At the first "Killer Kyle" golf tournament, I got reacquainted with many folks from Concord that I had not seen in a long time. One of those was Coach Friedl's son, Joe Junior. While talking with him, he said, "Danny, did you know that you were my hero while playing football at Concord?"

I responded, "I wish you had told me then, so I could have tried to be better." The message to all of us from this is to be the best that we can possibly be because we do not know who is watching!

Early in the spring of 1983, Mrs. Weaver went to the University of Virginia for a colon cancer surgery. About eighteen inches of large and small intestines were removed. The surgeon said that he took out all of the cancer and that she would not have to undergo radiation treatment nor have chemotherapy. During her stay in the hospital, Maxine and I drove from Manassas to Charlottesville, about two hours away, three times a week after teaching all day. A few days after her surgery and an exhausting day of teaching for us, we decided not to go to visit Maxine's mother. The good Lord sent us a message, "Go!" When we arrived at the hospital, a nurse met us and said, "Mrs. Weaver is not doing well. All of her vital signs are poor. She seems to have given up." She probably would have given up if we had not arrived when we did. A week later, she was discharged from the hospital. She was pitiful every time that we arrived. The word "cancer" frightened her because Mr. Weaver had died of cancer. She didn't seem to think that she would live.

After a long discussion of what to do, Maxine and I decided that we had to move to Culpeper to take care of her mother who had been living alone since Mr. Weaver died in 1976. In March, we put our beautiful fifteen-room house on the market to be sold. On the fifth day, our house sold with a full contract offer, although we had a fifteen inch snow on the ground when we listed it. We knew that we had to get busy locating a house in Culpeper.

Mrs. Weaver was very independent and Maxine is like her mother. We did not want to interfere with her independence, so we found a nice brick rambler at 1100 Fox Hill Lane with four acres of land. The view of Old Rag Mountain was picturesque, especially on clear days when we could see the sunset. When we moved there, we gave more care to Mrs. Weaver although I had a large yard to mow. I even planted a garden there although we still had one at the Weaver house. We carried "meals on wheels" to Maxine's mother many times. We also took her out to dinner on many occasions. She thrived on the attention.

When school started in the fall of 1983, Maxine and I traveled to Manassas since we had not changed jobs. We had to get up at five o'clock in the morning to be at work by seven-fifteen. My wife is not a morning person. I am glad that I was not a student in her first class each morning. I would drive to Stonewall Jackson High School which was about forty-five minutes from Culpeper, and Maxine drove across town to Osbourn Park High School which was another fifteen minutes. She picked me up at SJHS at three o'clock in the afternoon and then continued to drive to Culpeper while I slept. I listened to her say many times, "I can't keep doing this!" We had many chores at our home as well as taking care of Maxine's mother. We did not have much spare time for each other.

We transferred our membership from the Manassas Baptist Church to the Culpeper Baptist Church. We enrolled in a Sunday School couples' class taught by Joan Bloomer, a wonderful Bible teacher. We met many new friends, especially Faye and Shirley Gray, and Lynne and Dave Richardson. Joan was the principal of Culpeper County Junior High School. Her husband Jeff was an administrator in Prince William County Schools in Manassas. The Lord looked after us again as we were hired to teach in Joan's school the next year. Maxine taught ninth grade English and I taught physical science and coached track. Although we took a big cut in salary, we knew that Maxine's mother needed us more than we needed the money.

While living in Culpeper, I reunited with a friend Jack Fincham, whom I had played football with at

Culpeper County High School. He was a senior, and I was a freshman. He graduated from Virginia Tech and remains a loyal fan today. We became golfing buddies at the Culpeper Country Club along with Coach Shirley Gray who was wrestling coach and golf coach at Culpeper County High School. The second year in the Culpeper school system, Jack who was assistant principal at CCHS got me a job teaching biology and assistant coach in football and track at that school. Maxine remained as English teacher at the middle school. The head football coach at CCHS was Stan Wilson who knew a lot about coaching football but perhaps tried to teach too much to his players, which caused confusion. He had several assistants who thought they knew more than they did and a lot of coaching did not take place. The teams had average seasons but the high school wrestling team and golf teams were great. Coach Gray won several state championships while coaching each of those sports.

Coach Gray taught me how to play golf as I had played only a few times before moving to Culpeper. Maxine and I joined the Culpeper Country Club. We really couldn't afford it, but the Lord took care of us again. We needed $500 to join, but did not have the money. When we went to visit Maxine's mother, Mrs. Weaver asked, "Have you joined the country club yet?"

I said, "We do not have $500 to buy stock."

She seemed puzzled, then replied, "Guess what? I got a $500 check in the mail today. You may borrow it if you want."

I gladly took the money and joined the Culpeper

Country Club. For several years after Maxine and I married, we borrowed money from the Weavers and paid back over a period of time adding six percent interest. They helped us, and we helped them.

One of the loans that I had with Mr. Weaver was in 1967 when I bought seventy-six acres of land from him in Leon, Virginia. It was going to be our nest egg for retirement. In the 1980's, a neighbor offered me a great price for it, so I sold the Madison County land to him.

We had good neighbors on Fox Hill Lane. On the west side lived Dr. George Broman and his wife Nancy and on the north side, Dr. Al Cramer and his wife Linda. George was the team doctor for the athletic teams at CCHS as well as a surgeon at Culpeper Memorial Hospital. Al was my doctor after moving to Culpeper. He was also one of my golfing buddies, a hunting buddy, and a good friend.

When we moved to Culpeper, my heart had been "behaving itself."

One day after church, I felt faint with pains in my chest. Maxine took me to the Culpeper Memorial Hospital for tests. It was determined that I had a premature ventricular heartbeat. Al was not satisfied with the test results, so he ordered an echo cardiogram. It was then determined that there was a leakage at the mitral valve in my heart and leakage between the left auricle and left ventricle. He said to me, "Danny, it doesn't seem too serious now so we can postpone surgery for a few years." The Lord has worked in my life again. At this writing, twenty-two years have passed and I have not had surgery yet. I believe another miracle had happened in my life.

Shirley and I had many good golf matches. It took me forever to get good enough to beat him, which was not very often. He was quite a competitor and always liked to win. The only time he would coach me was at practice, not during a match. One day, Shirley and I were playing before his golf team started practice. It was a windy day and his golf team was sitting on the bench behind hole number nine, an uphill par-three hole. I was behind Shirley by two strokes when I hit my ball to the right and the wind was blowing my ball toward the hole to the left. His golfers jumped up and said, "It went in the hole!" Since I could not see the uphill green, I thought the golfers were playing a trick on me. Sure enough, it had gone into the hole. Shirley got a bogie an that hole, and I won our match by one stroke. Shirley said to me, "I hate to lose but do not mind getting beat with a hole-in-one!" Since then, I have had two other holes-in-one. The first one is registered at the World Golf Hall of Fame in St. Augustine, Florida.

Chapter Eleven

Good And Bad Years, 1990-1999

Early in 1990, Maxine's mammogram showed a lump in her left breast. Her surgeon told her that the whole breast and also the other breast which was cancer free should be removed, a double mastectomy. She saw another doctor for a second opinion. Since that was the standard procedure then, the second doctor recommended the double mastectomy. Maxine and I did quite a bit of research about breast cancer and the recommended procedure at that time. She still was not satisfied with the thought of removing a healthy breast, so she went to the third doctor in Richmond, Virginia. He explained that it was controversial during this time and he said, "I don't think it's necessary to remove a healthy breast." That's exactly what she wanted to hear!

The lumpectomy surgery was performed at Mary Washington Hospital in Fredericksburg, Virginia. It was a carcinoma in-situ, which meant that the cancer was self-contained and removed successfully. The surgeon said, "All of the cancer is removed and you won't have to undergo radiation or chemotherapy." The Lord had sent another miracle our way! Healing occurred and life finally got back to normal...whatever that is.

In the spring of 1992, A.T. Howard, my high school coach in football, basketball, track, and legal guardian, was voted into the Hall of Fame at Bluefield College in Bluefield, West Virginia. Maxine and I went to accept the plaque for him since he had died on March 13, 1965. (An interesting fact about his death on the thirteenth was that he was very superstitious and did not like the number 13.) We accepted the honor for him. He was recognized not only as a football player but also a football coach there. He was a great man who knew his football and had a compassionate heart for all his athletes.

In 1992, Maxine and I both retired from education. I had been in the field of education for thirty-five years and Maxine had been in it for twenty-eight years. She took off several years to raise our two girls. There were many interesting events in the classroom in which I could write several books!

One interesting story that I tell over and over is when I was giving a final exam in biology. As was my custom, I always walked around the room monitoring the class to determine that no one was cheating. Across the room, I noticed that a girl had a sheet of paper in her lap. She would look down at the paper, and then would write something on the test sheet. I went to her and said, "I'd like to see you out in the hall."

She looked at me in the typical way of innocence and said, "Why?"

"Please follow me out in the hallway as I want to talk to you." She followed me into the hallway. I asked, "Why were you cheating?"

With a feigned look of annoyance on her face, she said, "I was not cheating."

I said, "Why do you have a cheat sheet with you?"

"It is not a cheat sheet. It's a letter from my friend."

"I saw you cheating, so why don't you own up to it."

She said, "Mr. Crane, I would never cheat!"

This conversation was going nowhere so I asked, "Are you a Christian?" I thought that she would be truthful.

She responded quickly, "Oh, no! Mr. Crane, I'm a Baptist." At that point I knew she had a problem!

Several weeks after I retired, someone asked me, "Are you enjoying your retirement?"

It didn't take me a minute to answer, "I am having so much fun, I wish I had retired when I was twenty-one!"

That same year President-Elect Bill Clinton came to worship at the Culpeper Baptist Church. He was following the route that Thomas Jefferson had taken on his way to Washington, D.C. One of Clinton's famous stops was at our church. I was a deacon at the church and could not believe all of the preparation, not only at the church but also all over the town. There were numerous Secret Service Agents at church and around town. On Sunday when he and his family arrived at the church, snipers were stationed with their loaded weapons on top of all the tall buildings facing the church. There were many dog sniffing canines in the parking lot to make sure no explosives were there. Protestors were in front of the church with their large posters.

Maxine sang in the choir and had a "bird's eye view" of the hundreds in attendance. The church gave tickets to all members. People stood in line days before to get tickets. Some people that we had never seen before or since said, "We're members!" It was standing room only in the huge church.

When pastor Bert Browning began his sermon, he welcomed the Clinton group seated in the first four rows in the middle pew. He began by saying that the church will have to put a plaque on President Clinton's seat which will say, "President Clinton slept here in 1992." Clinton was very attentive and sang the hymns as if he were used to church hymns.

When the sermon was over, my job was to be a greeter at the exit that Bill Clinton would take to leave the church. When I shook his hand, I put my other hand on his back. One of the Secret Service Agents came running. When he realized no harm had occurred, he left without saying anything.

In 1992, at the last deacon's meeting, I was elected chairman for 1993. Prior to that, I was asked to run for chairman and I said that I did not want to run. Several weeks later, while sitting in my deer stand at Estil's farmhouse, where I was raised, the Lord caused me to think about the nomination. I decided that if I was approached again about the nomination for chairman, I would accept. I was asked again and was elected to that position.

When Maxine and I retired from our roles in education, we took many trips and bought many timeshares. One of my childhood dreams came true as we went to the Grand Ole Opry three times. I always wanted to perform on the stage at the Ryman Auditorium and I got the opportunity to do so. In fact, Maxine and I sang on the stage at the Ryman and when we finished, we got a standing ovation.

As Paul Harvey would say…now the rest of the story. We were on a bus tour of Nashville, Tennessee, and one of the stops was the Ryman Auditorium. Our guide asked us if we knew the song "You Are My Sunshine"? She told us to sing it and when we finished, applaud very loud. Then she said, "Now go home and tell your friends that you sang on the stage at the Ryman Auditorium in Nashville, Tennessee, and when you finished you got a standing ovation."

On our first trip to Nashville, we purchased another timeshare close to the Ryman. Several years later, a new manager stated, "I don't want to see too many gray heads on the stage nor in the audience." Maxine and I accommodated him as we traveled to Nashville and exchanged our timeshare to Myrtle Beach, South Carolina. We have not been to Nashville since and do not plan to go again.

In the spring of 1993, I was called to Rev. Browning's office for a meeting. He was one of the best preachers we have ever had. He told me that he was resigning as pastor of Culpeper Baptist Church to go to the Chesterfield Baptist Church outside of Richmond. I cried like a baby, another disappointment for me although I was happy for him.

The deacons searched for an interim pastor for the rest of the year. The acting pastor only had to be at the church two days a week so I had to perform duties such as visiting the sick, going to funerals and funeral homes. One night, I had to go to a family visitation and I went to the wrong funeral home. That family was so proud that I had come. After leaving that funeral home, I went to the correct one!

One day I went for a visitation at the Culpeper Memorial Hospital. When I stopped by the front desk, I recognized the name of a lady from our church. I located the room and saw that the black lady in the bed was not the member of our church. I had never seen her before. She said, "I was lying here praying that the Lord would send someone to my room to get my pocketbook out of the closet for me. It is in the top of the closet and I can't get out of bed." I had big goose bumps on my arms but carried on a conversation with her. Before I left, she said, "I knew that the Lord would answer my prayer." Perhaps I was an earthly angel for her that day.

In the spring of 1994, I was notified by Concord College that I had been voted into the first class of the Hall of Fame as an athlete. It was stated that Frank Parker, my college roommate and friend, had nominated me. The ceremony was to be held in the fall after one of the football games. Once again, the good Lord was working in my life.

When we arrived at Concord for the festivities,

Maxine and I went in the gym and did not see my retired jersey anywhere. We had not been to Concord in many years. My NAIA All-American football picture was hanging on the wall with the statistics I had at Concord, but no #28 jersey.

When the football team came through the parking lot entering the football field, Frank saw that a player was wearing #28 jersey. He stormed down to the field and told the football player to go with him to the head football coach, Bob Mullett. Frank told Bob that number twenty-eight jersey was retired and that the player could not wear that jersey. The young man went back into the gym with his coach and changed jerseys. Frank came to me in the bleachers, very upset, and told the story to me. I was not surprised, but upset. My question was, "How many times did a player from Concord wear #28 since it "got lost in the shuffle?" I was very angry and did not go to the football games for many years nor did I donate more money to them.

My wife Maxine, Cathie and her husband Bill Reel, their two sons Daniel and Aaron, Cheryl and her son Seth, and I went to the Hall of Fame dinner that night. Frank was giving the introduction of me and my accomplishments in football. He was still mad at Bob Mullett and the Athletic Director, Don Christie, for allowing a football player to wear my retired jersey. He looked at Don and Bob and said, "Did you all know that Danny Crane's football jersey was retired in 1956? I do not want to see or hear of any other football players wearing jersey number twenty-eight at any more Concord football games." He was very adamant about

116

that. I was somewhat embarrassed by that outpouring of disgust but went and accepted the plaque. I did not mention, in my acceptance speech anything about the jersey, but gave credit to several people who helped make me a good football player: Coach Friedl, Don Williams, Ray Halsey, A.T. Howard, Tom Atwell, and of course, Frank Parker. On the way out of the Banquet Hall, the young man who had been wearing jersey #28 came to me and said, "I'm sorry. I didn't know that your jersey had been retired."

I felt sorry for him and said, "Young man, it is not your fault for not knowing, it is the fault of the Athletic Director and the head football coach."

After several days of thinking and planning, I decided to write a letter to Bob Mullett and President Jerry Beasley explaining what had happened at the game and ceremony. Bob wrote a letter to me trying to explain why jersey twenty-eight was worn. He said that he had so many players, he was afraid that if he did not use twenty-eight, he would not have enough jerseys. He wrote in the letter that he wanted me to give permission to "un-retire your jersey" so he could have enough jerseys. What would you have done in a situation like that?

I spent several days seeking thoughts from my wife, family, and friends. I decided that I would not agree to "un-retire" my jersey. I wrote another letter to Bob Mullett and President Beasley explaining why I wanted the jersey to stay retired. I thought it was supposed to be an honor for the recipient and the school to have a jersey retired.

I received a very nice letter from President Beasley but never heard a word from Bob Mullett or Don Christie, but someone from Concord mailed me two #28 jerseys that were the Redskin colors, not the Concord colors. I gave them to our daughters Cheryl and Cathie.

About a year later, Ron Macosko became Athletic Director. Apparently someone told him about the problem of the retired jersey. Joe Friedl, Jr., son of my coach at Concord, became informed and took action. He bought a Redskin jersey #28 with the name "Green" on the back of it (Darryl Green's Redskin number) along with an old pair of football shoes which were not mine. Ron put that jersey in the trophy case in the gym with a note stating, "retired jersey of Dan Crane." The story does not end there! Ron remained at Concord several years but had to move on since his wife played professional golf with the LPGA group.

Maxine became a writer for the *Culpeper Magazine* in 1994 under the editor Donnie Johnston. After encouragement from her, I had several articles published.

While at Hilton Head Island in South Carolina for a Thanksgiving vacation, Maxine decided to play eighteen holes of golf. It was the first time that she had played and she wanted me to count every stroke. Guess what? Her score was 215, and it took two days to play eighteen holes. She wrote an article for the magazine entitled, "Culpeper's Worst Woman Golfer Tells of Good Times on the Links."

I will have to tell you some of that experience in

I ate enough breakfast to ensure me of not starving because I know it takes at least four hours to play 18 holes. I dressed in shorts and a cute little golfing shirt with a collar (all golfers know a shirt must have a collar.)

The day was a bit overcast. It matched my mood. "How can golfers get so excited about chasing that little ball all over the place?" I thought.

We arrived 15 minutes before our tee-off time. Danny loaded my gray and pink golf bag on the back of the cart. I unzipped a side pocket to find my newly purchased golf shoes with rubber cleats and a golf glove…

I stepped up to hole number one…I positioned my tee "dead center" between the ladies' red markers. I balanced a yellow ball on top of the tee.

I firmly planted my feet so that the left foot was on the left side of the ball and my right foot was on the right side of the ball.

I squatted slightly as I had seen a woman golfer on TV do.

I lowered my head. I planned to keep my eye on the ball.

The seven iron was raised and brought down quite rapidly behind the ball. The ball never went into the air, but it rolled about 80 feet down the middle. I was pleased!…

The second hole had a narrow fairway. A ditch filled with water was straight ahead…my ball plunked right in the middle.

On the next hole an alligator was sunning himself next to a stream of water. He was far to the left of where my ball should go. I missed the alligator. In fact I missed the
entire ball!

For the next several holes, my ball got into the air with a five iron. I discovered that I could really chip with a nine iron. My putting was pretty good. I was averaging 15-18 strokes for each hole.

Then it started to rain. Just a drizzle at first. I got up on the ninth hole. I mentally and physically went through my positioning techniques. I tried to incorporate all the advice I had heard that day. I hit the ball. It went about 30 feet. "Come get in the cart. I'll drive you to the ball." "No use." I muttered to my compassionate husband. 'I'll just walk that short distance and hit it again."

Danny was sitting in the sheltered golf cart. I was standing in the rain. I hit the ball with all my might. I didn't care how I positioned my body. My body was aching from all of the contortions that are "necessary" to hit the dumb ball…the ball had "sliced' or "spliced," or whatever. It zoomed diagonally to the golf cart and lodged under the accelerator. "Drive it to the green," I yelled. He didn't. I had to throw it into the fairway and hit it again…and again…and again…

On the last hole of that fateful day, I was exhausted. My back hurt. I was wet from the rain. I looked a mess. When that little white ball (the yellow one was in the water hole or on top of an alligator's head) dropped into the cup, I could have sung the Halleluiah Chorus…

When we got home the next Saturday, I dashed straight to the phone. I called our friend Shirley Gray, the high school golf coach.

"Guess what?" I happily exclaimed. "I played my first round of golf at Hilton Head."

"Great," he replied, "what did you shoot?"

"215."

Silence. An intake of breath. "Max, that's the worst score I've ever heard. Did you know that there's a tournament for the worst golfers in the country. I think you qualify."

Maxine has improved slightly, but she still doesn't play golf often.

In 1994, I became a member of the Hall of Fame in football and track in Culpeper and was nominated by Donnie Johnston, the publisher of the *Culpeper Magazine*. The other members are: Carter White, baseball; Herb Hash, baseball; Cindy Griffin, golf; Floyd Binns, coach; Kate Carter, coach. I do not know if anyone else had been named to the Hall of Fame since then. My wife and I live in North Carolina and cannot keep up with news in Culpeper.

Every time I came in from hunting, Maxine asked, "Did you catch anything?" One day I came in from hunting and she asked me that same question. I held up a completely whole deer tail and said, "I caught one by the tail and held on to it but it got away." I had shot the tail completely off a deer that was running through the woods. I tracked blood of the deer until the snow covered the trail. I never found the deer but hope that someone found and killed a bob-tailed deer soon after that.

Maxine got the wild idea to go hunting with me. She tagged along with me to Richardsville. It was a bitter cold day. I didn't think she would last long in the cold and I knew she couldn't stop talking long enough for me to see a deer. I found a perfect sawdust pile. I faced in one direction and she faced the opposite way. She was supposed to alert me if she saw anything, she refused to hold a gun.

We were not there long at all when she said, "I'm freezing."

After another five minutes, she wanted to go home, so we got all of our supplies together and left. I should have said, "What did you catch?"

She probably would have said, "A cold!" I never took her hunting again.

Maxine and I purchased several timeshares to be used for traveling. Timeshares are not an investment but they save one a lot of money if they are used or traded to be used at various locations. We have used timeshares in our travels from Maine to Florida, to California, and to Mexico.

Returning from one of our vacations in Myrtle Beach, Maxine and I had a flat tire on Interstate 95, just outside of Fayetteville, North Carolina. I was getting out the jack from the trunk when a state trooper pulled in behind us. He said, "May I help you?" The Lord had sent another angel, whose name was Joel A. Siles, to help us. He not only removed the flat tire and replaced the spare, but he also led us to the only service station open in Fayetteville that Sunday. Maxine and I decided to have four tires replaced rather than buying just one. Trooper Siles stayed with us until arrangements had been made to mount the tires so we could go back to Virginia. I wrote a letter to the State Police in North Carolina and explained how Mr. Siles had been so accommodating to us. I hope that he received great recognition for helping us that day.

In the middle 90's, Concord College began a program of selling bricks in honor or memory of someone. The bricks are placed on the walkway outside the library building. Maxine bought one in my honor stating that I was Concord's first NAIA All-American football player.

After retirement, I played golf for nineteen days in a row...rain or shine. It was becoming work for me since I was not getting any better. I sought some coaching from my friends, especially Shirley Gray. I finally became better as time went on. I played on the senior golf team at the Country Club of Culpeper. Luckily, I have had three holes-in-one. The latest was during a match with Fauquier Springs Country Club at Culpeper. They have a policy at the club that you have to "open the bar" when you get a hole-in-one. When I went by the club house, I opened the bar for everyone playing but limited it to one drink. I had "hole-in-one insurance" which amounted to two-hundred-fifty dollars. Guess what? Many players had more than one drink and the bar bill was five-hundred dollars. I hoped that I would not have another "hole-in-one." I have not had one since!

In 1999, our neighbor Dr. George Broman decided to run for the House of Delegates in Virginia. He asked Maxine and me if we would assist him in politicking for him. Since we had little or no skills in that, we told him we would do everything possible to help him get elected. That was a very busy year and Maxine and I learned a lot about politics and politicians. George had many experienced aides who helped him to get elected. After one term, George decided not to seek re-election. Maxine and I decided that we were glad that we had chosen the field of education as professions... not politics!

Chapter Twelve

Moving to North Carolina

Remember Y2K? It was supposed to be the year when the world would come to an end. Many reports stated that the rapture for Christians would occur. Nobody knew what to expect, but Maxine was storing food that we would need in an emergency, batteries in case we had no electricity, water in case we could not pump water, and anything else that she could think of to survive the unknown.

In the meantime, life went on without a hitch. Maxine and I were Sunday School teachers at Culpeper Baptist Church. Maxine was a choir member and served on many committees, including the Personnel Committee. I was a deacon for many years and the Chairman of the Deacons.

In February of each year for Valentine's Day, the Sunday School classes nominated a couple for King and Queen for the Sweetheart Banquet. The Sunday School classes planned the entire banquet. Invitations were sent out to all former kings and queens. One Sunday School class decorated the huge Fellowship Hall. A job that most classes disliked was planning the entertainment for the night. It was a busy time of preparation, but it was always a huge success.

The voting was a secretive task. The Sunday School classes voted and only the few who counted the votes knew who the King and Queen would be until the night of the Sweetheart Banquet. In February of 2000 Maxine and I were crowned King and Queen.

Several months later, Maxine had emergency surgery to remove an infected gall bladder. After several days in the Culpeper Memorial Hospital, I brought her home. She wasn't there long before I noticed that she was falling over in a faint. At the same time that she was fainting, the doorbell rang. It was our pastor Ted Fuson. I could not let him in because I was reviving Maxine. I drove her back to the hospital. This time she was diagnosed with pneumonia. She stayed four days in the hospital and then was allowed to come home and be treated by her husband and earthly angel "Dr. Crane"! It took awhile for her to recuperate.

Maxine grew up in a musical family. Her family owned an upright self-player piano which was too large for us to fit in our house. She wanted a piano so we purchased a beautiful computerized piano that could make any sound. We began to play music together. I decided that I needed a new guitar. Norval Waugh, who married my cousin Joyce, had played guitar music with me. He had a friend who owned the music store Pickers' Supply in Fredericksburg, Virginia. Norval accompanied me there to pick out a good guitar. After looking at many models, I found one that sounded great to me. It was a Taylor guitar and was quite expensive. The sale price was $2,000, but the owner said that he would sell it to me for $1,500. A sale was made and I was as happy as a dog with two bones. Maxine and I played quite often but there were some songs that I could not play since they had sharps and flats.

Norval came to my rescue once again. He taught me how to use a capo on the strings between the frets. By using that, I could play many songs. He was a very talented guitar player and an excellent teacher. He was also a Concord graduate and told me that he roomed in the same dormitory room that I had while I was at Concord. Norval was an excellent teacher and administrator for Prince William County Schools and Stafford County Schools for many years. After his retirement, he had open heart surgery and never fully recovered. At his funeral, his grandson used Norval's guitar to play a memorial to him.

Maxine and I started a singing group because we longed to hear the old hymns that were not being sung often in our church. We decided that we would get a group of four couples together to sing old hymns and gospel music. Maxine played the piano, Jim Knepp played the harmonica, and I played the guitar. We met at our house after the Sunday night church service. We always had prayer time, discussions concerning our church, and food that Maxine prepared. After several sessions and by "word of mouth," we grew to eighteen people.

A member of my Sunday School class had a book of gospel songs which he gave to us. His father had been a circuit riding preacher in one of the western states. We all agreed that our group would be called the "Circuit Riding Singers." We were invited to sing at several churches and many homes for the aged. They loved us at the homes because most of them could not see or hear very well!

The year of 2001 was the time for my fiftieth high school reunion. Bobby Loy, our class president lived in Charleston, South Carolina, and could not come to help organize the reunion. Since I was vice president of the class, I had to chair the planning sessions at our house.

In one of those planning sessions, we began to talk about our Christian faith. I told them that I was raised in a Methodist church, but after I married, I became a Baptist. John Russell Aylor said that it was the opposite for him. He said, "I was raised in the Baptist church but later I became a Methodist." He continued his story with the humorous statement, "When I was a child, I attended the Baptist church, including Sunday School. When I got old enough to realize what happened to John the Baptist, I decided to become a Methodist!" Naturally we all laughed at his humor.

In February of that year, Maxine and I used one of our timeshares and went to St. Augustine, Florida. I purchased enough vials of water from "The Fountain of Youth" for each class member to have as a souvenir at our reunion. They were such a hit that many class members wanted to know if we had any extra vials left over.

In the winter of 2001, while we were living in our brick Cape Cod house at 1100 Fox Hill Lane, we had a two-day snowfall of thirty-six inches. The blizzard was so bad that the wind blew drifts higher than the rooftops of our car and truck. It took me five days to shovel the vehicles out.

Ice covered the sidewalks. As I was walking out to get the mail, I slipped on the ice and fell backwards. The fall knocked me unconscious. When I came to, I called for Maxine since I could not get up. She did not hear me. I crawled up the three steps to the back door. I weakly knocked on the door leading into the kitchen. When Maxine opened the door, she screamed as she saw me lying on the steps.

Maxine called for the rescue squad. On the way to the hospital, an attendant tried to give me an IV, but he was never successful. At the hospital, after many X-rays, it was determined that nothing was broken. I had a concussion. Maxine enjoyed telling our friends, "The hospital staff X-rayed Danny's head and could not find anything in it so they sent him home!"

After that horrible blizzard experience, we decided to sell our house with four acres and move closer to town, closer to the hospital, and closer to Maxine's mother. We moved into a new house at 613 Country Club Road in the town of Culpeper.

I enjoyed being so close to the Culpeper Country Club. I bought a golf cart and on many occasions, I drove down to the Club to play golf. Late one summer afternoon, I headed to the golf course to play nine holes of golf. As I was going to hole number ten, I heard a weird sound in the woods next to me. When I looked to the right, I saw a huge tree falling right at the golf cart. I heard a loud crash, and I awoke lying on the ground somewhat dizzy. When I finally got up, I saw that the golf cart was positioned between the huge trunk of the tree and a very large limb. I do not remember turning the cart at all, but it had turned at a forty-five degree angle. If the cart had stayed on the path and gone straight ahead, I would not be living today. My heavenly angel had taken care of me once again. Many golfers heard the crash and came to see if I were okay. Nothing on my body was broken, but it took several days for me to get over the soreness.

Maxine's mother did not live with us in Culpeper. She remained in her house at 729 Sperryville Pike. She enjoyed shopping with Maxine and she always enjoyed the "meals on wheels" that Maxine took to her house. Although she was self-sufficient, I took care of her yard with the mowing of the grass, raking thousands of cones from the huge magnolia trees, and trimming the tall hedge. I also made paths for her when it snowed.

July 3, 2003, was a sad day. Maxine called Mrs. Weaver early in the morning. The phone rang and she did not answer. Maxine immediately left our house and hurried to her mother's house. She knew that something was wrong.

When Maxine entered her mother's bedroom, Mrs. Weaver was lying on the floor beside her bed. She had suffered a massive stroke.

Several years before that, I was talking to Mrs. Weaver about how long we wanted to live. She said, "I want to live until I am ninety-two, but then I think I will be done for."

She died July 6, at the age of ninety-one. She would have been ninety-two in November.

She had lived in the same house since 1935. She remained a sharp lady until the stroke took her life.

In the year of 2004, Concord College became Concord University. After several years, many of us who graduated from Concord College felt like we were forgotten graduates. The Athletic Department began an "Archives Room" under the gymnasium where many of the old records are kept. It is across from the weight room and dressing room, so it is not very accommodating for visitors. In fact, when I visited there in 2010, my retired jersey #28 was thrown in a corner with the name of "Green" on the back. In a conversation with Joe Friedl, Jr., I found out that he bought the jersey for the school because mine was "missing."

When my family visited in 2010, another retired jersey at Concord belonging to George "Joe Ed" Phillip #37, was in that room in a nice frame. When my daughter Cathie saw jersey #28 thrown in a corner in "the dungeon" she became very upset. Every college or university who has "retired jerseys" place them in the gymnasium and are very proud of the recipients. I spoke with the current Athletic Director Kevin Garrett and he assured me that the University would buy a #28 jersey and have it properly framed and displayed.

"Joe Ed" Phillips was an outstanding football player at Concord College in the late 1950's. In fact, he made the All-WVIAC football team in 1958, 1959, and 1960. His football jersey was retired in 1962. A couple of years later when Concord College became Concord

University, his retired jersey was "lost," just like mine! In my phone conversation with "Joe Ed," he told me that one of his friends at Concord had "seen a student" wearing his retired jersey on campus. "Joe Ed" was inducted into the Hall of Fame at Concord University in 2011..

The year of 2005 brought many major changes in our lives. My most important earthly angel, Maxine, and my heavenly angel work in many unbelievable ways. We were happily living in our retirement home at the Country Club of Culpeper. We loved it!

Maxine and I believe that the Lord works in strange and mysterious ways. Our younger daughter Cathie and her husband Bill Reel had two boys Daniel and Aaron who were attending Glenn High School in Kernersville, North Carolina. She wanted us to move to North Carolina to watch them participate in sports and music while they were still in school. She said, "It's time for you to be closer to us in North Carolina." During a visit to them in 2005, we were driving around looking at the sites when Cathie said, "Let me show you where Bill and I have a membership in a country club. It's more like a club in the country." We drove around in the Deep Springs County Club subdivision (which is in Stoneville) and saw a nice brick two-story home for sale.

The sign declared, "For sale. Call Don Warren." We did. Out of curiosity, we toured the house but it did not have a bedroom on the first floor. When we asked Don if he had any more houses for sale in the area, he said, "Let me show you one by the lake."

The minute we walked into the living room of that house, Maxine said, "I could live here forever!" The living room was paneled on two walls with many shelves for books and the view of the lake was spectacular.

We went home to Culpeper and put our house on the market for twice the amount that we had paid for it seven years before. We were still debating whether we should make the move to North Carolina. Maxine asked our older daughter Cheryl, "Do you mind if we move out of Virginia?."

Cheryl was teaching art in the Stafford County School System and enjoyed visiting weekly to eat Maxine's cooking. She didn't think that we really would move and she said, "It's fine with me, if that's what you want to do."

While I was debating the big move to another state, I went to the grocery store in Culpeper to pick up something for dinner. A song was playing "Going to Carolina in the Morning." I believe that the Lord told us that we had to move again.

Five days after listing our house with our realtor Dick Clore, we got a call that he had a full contract on our house in Culpeper. We accepted and called Don Warren in North Carolina and made an offer. We offered $15,000 less than the house was listed for and the owner accepted. Within four weeks from the time we viewed the house in Deep Springs for the first time, we were moving into it!

The people in North Carolina, especially in the Stoneville and Madison areas, are extremely friendly. Our neighbors across the street from us, the Aherons, are very special people. Steve was a builder for many years and now is a realtor. When I have a problem with our house, he comes over and fixes it. I try to pay him for what he does, but he always refuses any pay. He will not even let me pay for materials used. He and his wife Beth Anne and their son Justice, are fine Christian people and are a great help to Maxine and me. Other families on our cul-de-sac are the Rices, the Gordons, the Ogburns, and the McMichaels. We have met many good Christian friends at the First Baptist Church of Madison where we joined. Elnora Howell was instrumental in getting us to become members.

Chapter Thirteen

2005, Second Cancer Surgery

The year of 2005 was a trying time in my life and especially for Maxine. After getting her yearly mammogram, an invasive cancer was diagnosed in her right breast. Her surgeon, Dr. Fleishman recommended surgery to be performed on December 7. This date of December 7 was a good date and a bad date for me. The good part was that it was my mother's birthday. The bad part was that it was the date that Pearl Harbor was bombed by the Japanese which began World War II.

Dr. Fleishman was a well-respected surgeon at Morehead Memorial Hospital in Eden. Maxine had great confidence in him because he was very compassionate and was highly competent. She faced major surgery.

After asking the church and our friends for prayer, Maxine's surgery was performed. The lower half of her right breast was removed. Eight lymph nodes in her right arm were removed. It was discovered that no cancer was present in the lymph nodes. I praised the Lord for that! The oncologist recommended that she undergo radiation or chemotherapy . Maxine refused!

Everything that Maxine and I had read was questionable about radiation treatments for people over seventy-years-old. When she refused those treatments, the oncologist became upset. Maxine told him that Dr. Fleishman got all the cancer and that the lymph nodes were clear. She said, "It is my body and I can choose what to do with it. My doctor said that if the cancer comes back, he will remove the whole breast."

Just as I supported her during the first cancer surgery, I told her, "Whatever you choose to do, I will help you and support you one-hundred-percent."

Prior to this surgery, Maxine and I played a lot of tennis. In Culpeper, she played once a week all year long with a group of ladies. After this surgery, she was told that she could not lift anything with her right arm more than five pounds. If she did, she would have a risk of lymphedema, a severe swelling of the right arm. She was also told by her therapist that if she flew on a plane or played golf, she would have to wear an elastic sleeve on the right arm. She was devastated to learn that she would have to give up tennis.

I was glad that she could not play tennis anymore with me because she ran me to death. She expected me to hit the ball back to her and she would hit the ball on one side of the court and the next time on the opposite side. Many times after playing her, I felt like I had been in a track meet. Once as I was trying to return every hit, I injured my knee. After an MRI, it was determined that I had a torn meniscus in my right knee. After arthroscopic surgery, I was told that I had a bad case of arthritis and the bone had been scraped during surgery.

Maxine and I had to give up tennis!

Another repercussion from the cancer surgery for Maxine was that she had to be careful about pushing a vacuum cleaner with her right arm. I took over that duty most of the time.

As we got older, we always had a discussion on who was going to die first. I would say, "I want to die first!'

She said, "No, I want to die first." She always included with the remark, "I'll die when my mansion is ready."

One day I emphatically said, "I have to die first!"

She immediately questioned, "Why?"

"Because I have to get there first to vacuum your mansion!"

After we laughed about that, she said, "There'll be no dust in heaven!"

I've always loved telling jokes. One of my favorite is a football story. Two men were talking about heaven one day. They were great football players. They had played four years of high school football together, four years of college football together, and both had played professional football on the same team for years. They happened to move to the same town and remained close friends. As they aged, one day they began to talk about heaven. One said to the other, "Do you think they have football in heaven?"

The other said, "I don't know!"

"Let's make an agreement. The one who goes to heaven first will send back a message to the other as to whether they play football in heaven." An agreement was made.

One day not very long after that, one of the star football players died. He sent back a message to the other and said, "I have good news for you and bad news."

The other one said, "Give me the good news first."

The man in heaven said, "The good news is they do have football in heaven and the bad news is that you are the starting quarterback tomorrow!"

In talking about heaven, many times people don't remember what the Bible says about heaven or don't even believe in it. Many times when people talk about death, they cringe. Some people will say, "It is better to be over the hill than under it!" According to what I believe and read in the Bible, it is better to be "under the hill in heaven" than on earth. According to the apostle Paul in the NIV translation in the Bible, it is stated in Philippians 1:21-26: "For to me, to live is Christ and to die is gain. If I am to go on living in the body, this will mean fruitful labor for me. Yet what shall I choose? I do not know! I am torn between the two: I desire to part and be with Christ, which is better by far; but it is more necessary for you that I remain in the body. Convinced of this, I know that I will remain, and I will continue with all of you for your progress and joy in faith."

As Maxine was undergoing therapy three times a week for quite awhile, she began to get stronger physically as well as psychologically. She was always a fine Christian person much like her father, Elton Weaver.

As you can see, two of my earthly angels came from the same family. I loved my mother-in-law, Pansy Weaver, but I always tell Maxine that I am blessed that she was more like her father than her mother...bless her heart!

Maxine had always said, "The Lord sent us to North Carolina for several reasons...one being to find the correct surgeon to perform my cancer surgery."

About our marriage, she always said, "Our marriage was made in heaven and I have no doubt about that."

I always say, "Maxine chased me all over Germany and West Virginia before she finally snagged me."

I am very blessed to have such a beautiful, loving, caring, compassionate, Christian lady in my life. Last August in 2011, we celebrated fifty-three years of happy marriage.

Chapter Fourteen

Church and Golf in North Carolina

As time went on, Maxine and I became more involved in our church, the First Baptist Church of Madison. We had good Sunday School teachers. Maxine's teacher was Mabel Baird and mine was Lloyd Baird. Little did we know that both of them would soon retire from teaching Sunday School. Maxine became the teacher of her class of ladies and I became the teacher of Lloyd's class of men along with Leo Rhodes. Once again, we felt that the Lord had moved us to North Carolina for that purpose. Maxine participates in the choir and began a Bible Study class. She is also a member of a prayer shawl group of knitters who gave over one thousand shawls to the sick or to grieving individuals. Once a month when the shawls are completed, the church displays them and gives a special prayer for the recipients. Joyce Fulcher and Maxine were the only two women who could knit when they began in 2006. Now they have twenty very talented ladies.

I tried out for the choir, but I could not read music and as I say, "I did not make the cut." They sing very sophisticated music for a choir that numbers twelve. Other than teaching Sunday School, my main service to the church has been as a deacon.

We still miss our friends and family in Culpeper, but we have many good friends in North Carolina. We have a gang of birthday buddies: Mary and Herb Lewis, Omie and Joe Dillon, and Nancy and Barry Ellison. Not only do we celebrate birthdays, we play a lot of Mexican Train dominoes. Sometimes we take vacations together and have wonderful times.

One of the groups that I enjoy is the senior golfing group which Joe Dillon organized. It is a very diverse group and a very congenial group. We play golf three times a week, two at Deep Springs Country Club on Mondays and Fridays, and on Wednesdays we take a trip to other golf courses in the Greensboro and Winston Salem areas.

In Culpeper, my golfing buddy, Shirley Gray, played strictly by the rules. We could not roll the ball in the fairway and we had to putt out a hole, even if the ball was only one inch away from the cup. There were no "gimmies." It is different here. Our "old men" rules are as follows:

1. We tee-off from the senior tees.
2. If the golf ball is hit out-of-bounds, we go to where the ball went out-of-bounds, move it to the edge of the fairway, take a one-stroke penalty, and hit the ball.
3. The ball can be rolled one club length inside the tree line including the rough.
4. We play a point system as follows:

-a birdie is 4 points

-a par is 2 points

-a bogie is 1 point

-a double bogie is 0 points

-a triple bogie is minus 1 point

-a maximum of 2 triple bogies is allowed on each nine holes

5. To determine how many points one has to make, his handicap is subtracted from 36 and that would be the number of points he would have to make. For example, If my handicap were 22, I would subtract 22 from 36 and get 14; therefore, I would have to make 14 points, 7 on each nine holes to get an even score. The person or team with the most points wins. The bet is one-dollar on the front, one-dollar on the back, and one-dollar overall. The most one can lose is three dollars.

6. Teams are divided into singletons, twosomes, threesomes, or foursomes depending on how many seniors show up that day.

7. Teams are determined by putting one's golf ball in a hat and drawing out balls.

Most of the time, our senior group has at least twelve players and even at times, we have had as many as sixteen players. We enjoy our fellowship more than how we play golf. When I came back from golfing today, I told Maxine, "I am not a good golfer and never will be." I can shoot 80 one day and two days later shoot 100, but I enjoy the fellowship and the exercise. At our age, we're thankful that we can play...whatever the score happens to be.

Epilogue

Growing up without a Father has not been easy. There were many times in my life when I questioned, why me? Several days ago someone asked me if I ever blamed God for what happened to my father. I told him that I tried to move on and not blame God. Ray Tolson, who was my Sunday School teacher in Woodbridge, Virginia, told us to never blame God when bad things happen to good people. In fact, he told us that when he died he would ask God why certain things happened in his life. The Lord has been quite busy listening to him as Ray went to meet the Lord several years ago.

The advice that I can offer to those who grow up without a Father is to keep a strong faith in God. The times that I turned my back on God were not very happy. Regardless of what happens in life, keep your Christian faith in God. When someone says, "God and I do not have a close relationship," you might ask, "Who moved?"

Motivation is the key to all phases of life. Try to use all of your body and soul to honor God in all that you do. As I told all the athletes that I coached, "Every time you play a game, try to be better than the last time you played." Our lives should be lived in such a way that we will be better tomorrow than we are today. Honor the good Lord in all that you do.

Writing this book has brought back many memories while growing up without a Father. The most important encouragement I received from many coaches was "never give up." Winston Churchill made one of the most important speeches, and perhaps the shortest, when he said, "Never, never, never give up."

Grantland Rice, one of the most prominent sports writers in the United States wrote, "When the Great Scorer comes to call your name, it does not matter whether you won or lost but how you played the game." All of us must remain in good mental and physical shape because we may become the starting quarterback tomorrow.

I hope you will enjoy this book and that you will also be aware of your earthly angels and heavenly angels. They will encourage you when things seem too hard to handle.

My Turn!!

By Maxine Weaver Crane

In July of 2011, I taught a writing class at the Germanna Reunion in Orange County, Virginia. This is the exact location that my German ancestors landed by ship in 1717. The first colony of Germans arrived in 1714. Descendants congregate there every July for a family reunion. They come from many states in the United States and Germany. It is a well-organized weekend of tours, instructional sessions, and great fellowship with relatives.

My goal in teaching "How to Write Your Story" was to inspire the approximately sixty members in my class to write about a member of their family. Many have been studying their genealogy longer than I have. They are usually willing to share their research with their current "cousins." After instructing them on the way to write their stories, I asked them to return to the next reunion with a biography that we could file in "The Memorial Foundation of the Germanna Colonies in Virginia."

This year will be the 55th Annual Conference

and Reunion celebrating "The Women of Germanna." Once again, I am teaching a class on "How to Write Your Story" on July 14. (For more information on Germanna, visit the website www.germanna.org)

I did not realize that my husband (who was in the class last year) would get motivated to write his story. For many years I tried to get him to write his story as a legacy for our children Cheryl and Cathie; our grandchildren Seth, Daniel, and Aaron; and our great-grandchildren Steven and Cheyenne.

He always replied, "I don't want them to think that I'm bragging."

Every time he said this, I would reply, "When you die, your story will die."

As a teacher of English for twenty-eight years, I always encouraged my students to write. Each year I submitted their writings to newspapers, magazines, and literary contests.

Some students would complain and say, "I can't write!"

My answer was, "Can you talk on a phone? If you can talk, you can write!" I became their cheerleader by constantly encouraging and saying, "You can do it!"

When I retired from teaching high school English for twenty-eight years, I decided it was time for me to write a story. I became very interested in a lady named Frances Henderson. She was left with Alpha and Fountain Deale by her mother in 1846. Mrs. Henderson was traveling on foot from Virginia to Missouri. She stopped at a pre-civil war home in Madison County and asked if they would keep Frances. Alpha and Fountain Deale agreed to take her as a companion for their daughter Sarah. Frances' mother said, "Keep'er in dis house in case I ever come back." She turned to her daughter and said, "Don't ya ever ask for nothing."

The next two owners also stored wills in their Bibles. They wanted Frances Henderson to be in the house when her mother returned for her. Mrs. Henderson never returned for Frances. Frances became loved and respected by three owners of that house until she died February 28, 1925. She was eighty-four-years old. Every person that I interviewed said, "She was a sweet lady who never asked for nothing."

I wrote for days, weeks, months…forever it seemed. I would awaken in the morning and think, "What will Frances do today?" Since I did not know her, I had to create her story based on the history and current events of 1846-1925 and the interviews and notes that I had taken for thirty years.

My greatest source for facts was my aunt Mae Yowell. She was born in 1915 and lived in the farmhouse with Frances. I called many times to ask about the seven children of Sarah and Rowland Yowell or the ten children of Elizabeth and Henry Weaver. She always had clever stories. Her memory is unbelievable. At the age of ninety six, she has a tremendous memory and a great wit. I always tell her, "If the people of the world were like you, there would never be wars or hatred."

My husband was my motivator to complete the book. It takes a lot of time and effort to complete a book. One morning I said, "I don't think that I want to complete this book. Who will be interested?"

Danny proofed each page as I completed it. The day that I was questioning whether to complete it, he was reading about the death of Henry Weaver. When I insinuated that I was not going to finish it, he said, " If you can make me cry, a dumb old football coach, you are a good writer and you should complete this book." It became a team effort after that...I wrote daily and he proofed each page.

Our daughter Cheryl illustrated my book with sketches of 19th Century homes and artifacts that are unfamiliar in today's society. She teaches art in Stafford County, Virginia.

The book is currently in the second printing with a limited number of copies left. With Danny's permission, I am supplying you with the first chapters of my book. If you are interested in ordering a copy of my book, an order blank is at the end of this book.

ASK FOR NOTHING
A TRUE STORY
1846-1925

By Maxine Weaver Crane
Illustrated by Cheryl Crane

Chapter One
1846

Night was approaching fast. The air was unusually cold for October. Ma Henderson looked down in the valley and saw a frame house nestled near a stream. She was traveling with a horse-drawn cart and knew that the horse needed a break. She opened the gate leading off the main road and started down the lane to the house. As she got closer, she noticed a spry little lady leaving the lower level of the house.

Ma Henderson stopped at the branch and let the horse get a drink. Then she cautiously stepped over the rocks that had been evenly placed over the branch. She led the horse and wagon to the house.

"Hullo," yelled the little lady. "Can I hep you?"

"Yeah, I'm comin' quick as I can," called Ma. By the time she got to the yard gate, a heavyset man appeared in the yard. He could see that possessions were stacked high on a small wagon. Children were under the canvas on the wagon. He couldn't see the faces of the children, but he quickly surmised that the woman was running away from something.

Fountain Deale was the owner of approximately 500 acres of land in Madison County, Virginia. His ancestry could be traced to the Germanna settlement near Culpeper, Virginia. He and his wife Alpha were used to people wandering into their land. Nomads either crossed Deale Mountain from the west or came by Duet from the east. Hardly a week passed without someone asking for a meal or something. He was not surprised by this woman and a cart filled with children and possessions.

"Coulda' have sump'n for the chillun in the wagon?" she asked. "I been onna road all day. They needs water."

Alpha darted back into the house. Fountain said, "Come in. Just et suppa. Got some ash cakes and beans left over. Yore welcome."

Ma Henderson was hesitant but she knew she'd be walking all night. Her children could use food and a break. "Okay," she shyly stated, "but jest for a spell."

When they got inside the kitchen, Ma Henderson noticed an oak rectangular table in the middle of the kitchen. Twelve people could easily sit around it. Benches were pushed under the table. The fireplace glowed with embers of a dying fire. The iron pot had been pulled from the fire and the beans were cooling. Eleven-year-old Sarah rocked quietly next to the fireplace.

Alpha set a plate of ash cakes on the table. She placed a plate in front of each guest. Then she ladled beans onto each plate.

"Gurls, bow yore heads a'fore we eat." The three skinny little girls bowed their heads and listened as a Dutch prayer was given by Ma Henderson. The children ate heartily. Ma tried to disguise that she was

151

hungry. She ate cautiously and gratefully for each bite.

Sarah, the daughter of Alpha and Fountain, couldn't understand a word of the Dutch prayer. She watched as the children and their mother devoured left-overs. She rocked back and forth in a child's oak rocker and watched without saying a word.

Sarah noticed that one of the children was very small. She had straight brown hair that hung to her shoulders. Her eyes looked too large for her body. She heard Alpha say, "What's yore name, honey?"

"Frances," she responded. After looking into the eyes of Alpha, she looked back at her empty plate.

Ma Henderson looked at Alpha and said, "She ain't right. I'm tryin' to git to Missouri and I'll never git there wid her. She's been slowing me up ever since we left home yestiddy. Ya got sucha big house. Could you take Frances off'n my hands? I gotta move on." She looked pleadingly at Alpha.

Alpha looked again at Frances. She had the sweetest angelic face. Alpha fell in love with her immediately. "What ya mean ain't right?"

"Frances was born 'tarded. Slow to speak. Slow to larn. Never will get larnin' from nobody."

"You mean you'd leave her here?" Alpha couldn't believe that a Mother would leave a child with strangers. She looked at Sarah and thought, "I'd never let Sarah outta my sight."

"On one condition," said Ma Henderson. "She must allus be in this house. If'n you sell, she stays. Put it in yore will. Who knows...I might come back."

Five-year-old Frances watched her mother leave.

Her sisters were crying unashamedly as they sensed the loss of their little sister. Ma Henderson quickly ushered the girls out into the night.

At that moment Frances didn't realize that her family had left her. Her eyes were still focusing on the pleasant kitchen. She saw without understanding that the north wall was constructed of rock mortised with mud and lime. It was eighteen inches thick and was underground which helped with warmth in the winter and coolness in the summer. The floor was dirt. Large hand-hewn timbers were overhead and were held together with wooden pegs. Each timber was numbered with Roman numerals. The front of the kitchen was ground level. Frances looked at the door. "Whar'd they go?" Frances' eyes brimmed with tears as Alpha explained, "They gone. Ya our lil' gal now."

Sarah took her cue from her mother, "Frances, I'll lead ya upstairs."

It was dark and cold outside. The house was built with no interior steps leading from the kitchen into the main part of the house. They had to go outside in order to get upstairs to the front room. Sarah led Frances up the wooden steps outside, through the front door, and into the front room. Frances looked around. A fire burned in the fireplace. There were two windows on the north and south sides of the room. A tiny window was next to the fireplace that faced east. High-backed rockers were positioned around the room with white crocheted covers on the backs of each chair. It was a cozy room, but Frances was with strangers.

When Alpha entered the front room, she noticed

that Frances was nodding. "Frances, I know yore tired. It's 'most eight o'clock. Let me show you your room." Alpha stood and beckoned for Frances to follow.

The steps were so wide and tall that Frances had a tough time keeping up. When they got to the top of the stairs, Alpha pointed to the right and said, "Me and Fountain sleep there." She pointed to the left and said, "You and Sarah'll share that room."

The room looked huge. It was cold because a fire was not in the fireplace. There were two windows with white flimsy curtains. One large oak bed seemed to encompass the room.

"Under yore bed is a slop jar. If ya pee in it, it's yore job to empty it and wash it. Here's a gown that's Sarah's. Put it on. Water's in the bowl and pitcher. Use it. I'll empty it in the morning." She left the room.

Frances walked over to the bed. It was too tall. She couldn't decide how she'd get in it. "I gotta do things right. I gotta be good."

She pulled the slop jar out from under the bed. With the thoughts of having to empty it the next morning she thought, "I won't pee. I'll hold it." She couldn't reach the washcloth or towel hanging on the oak washstand so she thought, "Can't be a bother. I'll wash later."

She was so tired. The trip had been long. "I gotta manage. Ma told me not to ask for nothing."

After tucking her toes onto the side of the bed, on her fifth try she made it into the feather tick. Sarah watched. She was apprehensive about sharing her bed, but she was happy to have a little sister. Most families in the area were large and she wanted a brother or sister so she could be like the other families.

Frances rolled back and forth several times. The crunching of the straw mattress under the feather tick kept her awake. The shadows on the wall seemed to ominously threaten her. She felt entombed with the feather ticking all around her. She shut her eyes to keep out the spooks and within minutes, she was sound asleep.

Alpha and Fountain sat quietly in the front room. Fountain was peeling an apple with his pocket knife.

"Ya sump'n Fountain," said Alpha. "I ain't never seed another soul who could peel an apple that a'way. I allus break the peel somewhar."

Fountain threw the one long continuous peeling into the fire. "Alpha, right tanight we gotta do what Ma Henderson said. We gotta make a will. Git my writin' tablet."

Alpha obediently took the tablet and pencil to Fountain. "Yore right. We gotta protect that lil' gal."

Fountain wrote in longhand. "I Fountain Deale born January 11, 1809 aged 37 and Alpha Hoffman Deale born April 1, 1811 aged 35 do hereby decree that upon our deaths Frances Henderson must remain in this house at the foothills of Deale Mountain." He signed it October 10, 1846.

"Should we spell Deale Mountain without the 'e' in it?"

"Naw," stated Alpha. "That's tha way it's allus been. Leave it, but let's drop tha 'e' in our names. Most folks change name spellin' all tha time." " A l - pha, put this inna good place. That lil'un needs protec-

155

tion. We'll keep 'er as long as we kin. Then whoever buys this house from us will git Frances, too."

Alpha took the paper and read the will. "How 'bout adding if'n they don't keep 'er, they'd hafta pay 'er fifty dollars a year fa tha rest of 'er days?"

"That's a good idee. Nobody around here makes fifty dollars a year so's they'd hafta keep 'er." He licked the end of his pencil and added, "If you don't keep her in this house, you shall pay her $50 a year the rest of her life."

Alpha took the handwritten will and placed it in the family Bible.

Chapter Two
1846

Frances was so excited. It was November 16, her sixth birthday. As a gift to her, Sarah promised that she would take Frances to school with her. Frances' feet hit the cold floor but she didn't feel the cold. She rushed to the washstand, took her washcloth off the towel rack, and washed her face quickly.

"Sarie, will the teacher whup me?" She had heard stories about the teacher hitting children with a hickory stick.

Sarah was five years older than Frances. She had described everything about school to Frances, but she patiently answered, "She only hits those who's bad. Yore never bad."

"How far'll we walk? Wear boots? Eat lunch?" Frances fired one question after another.

"Frances, git dressed. Put on a clean dress and warm socks. Wear yore new boots that Pa bought ya. Come on. Ma's got breakfast. I kin smell bacon cookin' already. 'member chillun are to be seen and not heard. Don't ask Ma a bunch o'questions."

They scampered out of the bedroom, down the long flight of stairs to the front room, and then out the front door. Neither felt the cold air as they ran from the November chill into the kitchen.

Ma was setting plates heaped with food onto the table. Fountain was already seated at the head of the table. "Mornin' gurls. Ready for school, Frances?"

Frances remembered to "be seen and not heard" so she shook her head in an affirmative nod.

"Sarah, you look afta Frances. If tha teachar'll let her stay, she kin go ever'day."

Frances was so fidgety that she had a hard time concentrating on breakfast. She couldn't wait to see other children and the one-room school that Sarah had described to her last night. She had never seen a teacher so she didn't understand that part of education.

"Keep yore new boots on yore feet all tha time," said Alpha. "It's time to go. Sarah, don't let Frances outta yore sight."

"Okay, Ma." Sarah grabbed her lunch pail and handed the other one to Frances. Alpha had packed bacon on biscuits, a jar of fresh milk, and a sugar cookie in each pail.

Frances was elated to carry the little tin pail with a top on it. She couldn't wait to see what was inside.

They headed out the yard gate. "Frances, hold my hand all the way to school. When we get there, I'll set you in one of the desks up front. The lil' uns set up front. I'm bigger. I set about halfway back in the room. Older chillun' set farther back. There's a big stove at tha front. The teachar'll have a hot fire by the time we git thar. Don't tetch it. It'll burn thar gloves right off'n yore fingas."

Frances was trying to keep up the pace with Sarah and was listening to every word of instruction. She once again remembered the words of her ma a month ago..."don't ask for nothing." She tried to follow those parting words.

The chill in the air was making Frances' nose red and it began to run. "Frances, blow yore nose on yore hankie. You don't wanna go in school wid yore nose drippin' all over da place."

While they were hurrying down the one-lane road to school, the school teacher was fixing the fire. Several older boys were bringing in firewood and stacking it next to the potbellied stove.

Frances' heart was flopping in her chest as they arrived at the front door of the school. Partly it was from moving so fast in the cold, but mostly it was from the excitement of being in school with Sarah on November 16, her birthday.

When Frances stepped inside the room, she saw big children, middle-sized children, and little children. Sarah led her to the front of the room. "Teachar, this here is Frances. She is six years old taday. Can she set in school with me taday?"

The teacher looked at the frail little girl. "Sure. Frances, sit in the front row next to the fire. I know you are cold after walking all the way to school."

"Children, we have a new member in our class today. This is Frances Henderson. She lives with the Deals. Make her welcome. Today's her birthday."

The teacher said, "Take out your slates. I want you older children to use Walker's Dictionary and write the definition for the word "legend." She went to the blackboard and printed the word 'legend.' You older children will plan a legend that you can tell to the class." Fingers eagerly flipped through the dictionary until they found the word "legend" and they busily copied all of the information including the parts of speech, synonyms, antonyms, and several definitions.

"Mam," hollered a huge husky-looking boy from the back of the room. "I know a good 'un. I cain't write. I kin tell it right now."

"Okay, Rufus, after lunch we'll let you tell the legend that you know."

Frances tried to draw the letter "L." She made a big line down the slate that was on her desk. The line was slanted rather than straight. When she drew the second part of the letter, it was more in the middle of the line than at the bottom of the letter. She was so proud. "I done it!" she thought. She was ready to try the next letter when the teacher said, "You children who have McGuffey's First Eclectic Reader, turn to page 59. Today you will be on lesson 44. Read the words with me...school, room, even, three, small, book, rude, teacher, reading, noon, poor. Pay attention to the phonics key over each word. Read the story on pages 59 and 60 silently. I will listen to each one of you as you read to me during the day."

"One group is finishing McGuffey's Reader today. Turn to page 93. Listen as I read the last two pages of Lesson LXIII." Sarah and three other children turned to page 93 and listened as she read, "We have come to the last lesson in this book. We have finished the First

160

Reader. You can now read all the lessons in it, and can write them on your slates. Have you taken good care of your book? Children should always keep their books neat and clean. Are you not glad to be ready for a new book? Your parents are very kind to send you to school. If you are good, and if you try to learn, your teacher will love you, and you will please your parents. Be kind to all, and do not waste your time in school. When you go home, you may ask your parents to get you a Second Reader."

Sarah was so proud that she had completed the entire reader. She knew that her parents would be happy to get the next book for her. Someone in the neighborhood would have a copy that she could borrow.

The teacher was moving from desk to desk observing all of the pupils at work. Frances heard her ask Johnnie to name some words that started with the letter "L." He slowly pronounced each syllable, "ladder,,, leader…lard… lazy… lion…lunch…I'm starved!"

She looked at her watch. It was almost noon. "Okay," she said, "take out your lunch pails. We'll have lunch and then you'll have recess for an hour. We'll have our blessing for the food before we eat. Bow your head, Frances." She made sure that every head was bowed and every eye was closed and then she repeated her favorite blessing, "God is great. God is good. Now we thank him for our food. By His hands we are fed . Give us Lord our daily bread. Amen."

The children lifted the tops of their desks and took out their lunch pails. Frances was starved. She ate the biscuit, drank the milk, and ate the cookie. After she ate, the warmth of the fire beside her made her so sleepy that she put her head on the desk and went straight to sleep.

The older class members were outside. The boys were shooting marbles on the sunny side of the building. The girls were chatting. The younger children were playing dodge ball and bullying each other.

The teacher tapped Frances on the shoulder, "Frances, you need some exercise. Put on your coat, hat, and gloves and go outside for awhile. Don't forget to visit the outdoor johnny house before you come in."

Frances rubbed her eyes. She got up and scurried outside. "I gotta obey," she thought. When she got outside, she noticed that Sarah was with friends so she sat down on the school steps and watched.

After recess the thirty pupils were seated once again from the smallest to the largest. Rufus was seated on the back row. He stood up and shouted, "It's afta lunch. I wanna tell my legin."

"Okay, Rufus, come to the front of the room."

Rufus ambled to the front. He smacked a couple of boys on the head as he passed. He pulled a couple of pigtails as he passed the girls. "My story's 'bout injuns..." He enjoyed all of the eyes that were on him. "Injuns was in Madison on this very spot. They used rocks and made spears to hunt and kill people. They'd scalp tha hair off'n yore head in a minute." He raised his long hair and demonstrated.

This story scared Frances. She visualized the Indians coming out of Deale Mountain one night to get her. She put her hands over her ears. She didn't want to hear anymore of that legend.

That afternoon on the way home Sarah said, "Don't pay no 'tenshun to Rufus. He's all mouth."

When they entered the kitchen, Frances saw a chocolate cake in the middle of the table. It had six candles on the top. Frances' eyes opened as far as they could and she screamed, "Fa me!! It's fa me?" S h e had never seen such a beautiful cake. The icing was white and the candles were pink. She clapped her hands and smiled her biggest smile at Alpha. Alpha hugged Frances and said, "Tanight we'll celebrate your first birthday with us. We're so happy yore with us."

Sarah hugged Frances and said, "Frances, ya my lil' sister."

Chapter Three
1846

Frances was awakened suddenly with the worst squealing that she had ever heard. The keening sound pierced her ears and made the hair stand up on her arms. "Sarie, Sarie, wake up. Whut's dat? I'm skeered!"

Sarah rolled over and faced Frances. "Frances, taday's hog killin' day. The men 're catchin' tha hogs right now to kill 'em. The women folks 're gatherin' in the kitchen for a hard day's work. We gotta hep. Cold weather's here to stay so's safe to cut up all that hog meat and keep it 'til spring. You ain't lived 'til you eat fresh hog meat."

All farmers helped each other in late November to kill hogs. The neighboring farmers congregated at the Deal's house early that morning. A fire burned heartily under a huge scalding tub in the backyard. The weather was a perfect thirty-two degrees with no clouds in the sky.

During the year Fountain's hogs roamed in a large pen in the mountain where they could drink from the branch and eat acorns and chestnuts. By the first of November, Fountain penned them into a smaller area and fed them corn to fatten them. He believed that acorns gave the fat on hogs a bitter taste and that corn made the lard sweeter.

"Larkin, we're ready for the first 'un," Fountain called to his brother. Larkin and his helpers wrestled the first hog onto the ground and cut the jugular vein. When the bleeding slowed, the four men placed the 350 pound hog in the scalding pan. "Careful, "Fountain called, "don't burn yo'selves."

A cable was under the hog in the scalding pan to help the men pull it out and onto a platform for scraping. Several men and even small boys scraped the hair off the hogs by using gray zinc canning jar lids and butcher knives. Sometimes a hog was dipped several times to remove all of the hair.

Frances had been told not to go into the backyard. Her curiosity got the best of her. After breakfast the women folks were cleaning everything off the kitchen table, stirring the fire, and readying themselves for their roles of the day. No one noticed as Frances went out the back gate. She saw a hog hanging from a sturdy limb on a walnut tree. The huge hog was suspended so that the head was facing the ground. Without hair on the hide, it shone in the sunlight. She saw men scraping the hair off another hog. Then she witnessed an awful sight. A young boy was pulling toenails off a hog when the hook slipped and slit his hand deeply. Frances could see blood running down his arm. One of the farmers acted quickly. He poured turpentine on the cut. Then he tied a white rag around the hand and said, "Git back to work. It'll git well 'fore ya git married."

The men worked with skill and precision. Every

part of the hog was used for something. Nothing was wasted. Even the intestines were cleaned in the branch for a future chitterling supper.

The scene became too much for Frances. She thought that she would be sick if she watched another minute. She scampered back toward the house and into the kitchen.

"Frances, whar ya been?" Alpha saw the white-faced youngster enter the kitchen. "It's time for us'uns to git to work. Here's yore job." She stretched a long piece of fat on the table and handed Frances a knife. "Be keerful. Cut the fat inna small chunks. Throw them chunks in this pan here. We cook it down fa cracklin' and lard."

While she was showing Frances how to cut the fat, Fountain brought a huge pan of tenderloin, hearts, lungs, livers, and kidneys for the women to store in the icehouse or to cook that day. Alpha said, "Thanks, Fountain, the faster we put it up, the betta it'll be."

Frances heard Alpha say that they would can the backbones, ribs, and sausage the next day. She knew that she and Sarah wouldn't have time to play for another day. "I laks to play. This here's hard work," she thought as she cut the fat into small hunks.

Sarah saw the frown on Frances' face and asked, "Frances, did ya folks butcha hogs?"

"Naw."

"Do ya know what we do wid all this meat?"

"Naw."

"We eat it silly. All year long. Tha icehouse holds some 'til spring. Some's canned. Tha rest is put

166

in the meat house that's behind this house."

Sarah went over to a shelf in the kitchen and pulled off a cookbook. "Listen and I'll read ya what they do. Ma's got a book. She don't use it much. She knows how ta do it all."

Sarah had a captive audience. The women were so busy that they didn't notice the two girls reading from a worn book that Alpha had painstakingly copied from her ma's recipes years ago. Sarah knew that Frances would never be able to read, so she showed her the words as she read. She skipped the part about making souse and scrapple out of the hog's head. She also skipped the recipe for hog's head stew. She skipped the part about jowls, tongue, brain, snout, ears, liver, heart, lights, stomach, and intestines. Finally she decided that she could safely read about the feet. She knew that Frances would like pig feet. Frances loved chicken feet. When Alpha fried chicken, she'd fry the feet first. Frances and Sarah would stand on the porch and eat the fried chicken feet while supper was cooking.

"Wait 'til Ma cooks pig feet. She cooks 'em most of tha day. When we eat 'em fa suppa, tha skin falls off'n tha bones. We put vin'gie all over 'em. Yum!" Then she proceeded to read recipes using the backbone, ribs, tail, and sausage.

Frances was getting bored but Sarah continued to educate her by telling how the other meat was kept. "Tha men work all day cuttin' up the hog. They cut hams from the hind parts and salt 'em so's they's white with salt. Then they cut the shoulders from the front part of the hog and salt 'em. They store the hams in wooden boxes in the meat house. They salt and hang the shoulders from the rafters so's they kin cut bacon to fry fa breakfast. They hang side meat or middlin' so's they can cut off hunks for Ma to cook with beans."

Sarah was going to tell Frances how they made soap from lard and many other things, but Frances was falling asleep.

"Sarah, don't be idle. Git back to work." Alpha took the recipe book from Sarah and put it back on the kitchen shelf.

After all the neighbors left late that afternoon, Alpha and Fountain were both exhausted. Alpha knew that she still had supper to prepare. Earlier in the afternoon she had put potatoes in the coals in the fireplace to bake. A big pot of canned green beans was cooking over the fire. "Gurls, set the table for suppa. I'm fryin' fresh tenderloin."

Frances couldn't wait to taste the fresh meat. Sarah had told her how wonderful it tasted. She watched Alpha dip the slices of meat in flour and put them in a frying pan that was bubbling with hot lard over the fire. Salt and pepper were heavily applied to each slice. As the chops fried, the aroma was so scintillating that Frances didn't think she could wait. She kept walking from the fireplace to the table and back again. She sat in the rocker and rocked back and forth. Her mouth was watering and her stomach was growling.

Finally the food was on the table. The girls sat on one side of the table. Fountain was at the head of the table and Alpha sat at the foot of the table which was near the fireplace.

"Bow ya heads for grace," Fountain solemnly declared. "Lawd, thank ya for all this bounty. Thank ya fa fine neighbors who done holp us today. Let this be nourishment to our bodies and strength to our souls. In Jesus' name. Amen"

Frances ate so much her stomach hurt. She couldn't wait to crawl into bed. The day had drained her physically and mentally.

When she and Sarah arrived at their bedroom, the room was ice cold. Alpha had placed a heated flat iron on Sarah's side of the bed and one on Frances' side of the bed. Each iron had been carefully wrapped in cloths so the girls would not burn their feet.

Frances opened her dresser drawer and took out her woolen gown. She slipped it quickly over her head and leaped into her side of the bed.

As she pulled the quilts over her head, she quietly whispered to Sarah, "Sarie, Sarie, I don't lak hog killin' days."

"Me, neither," came the instant reply.

ORDER FORM

For a complete copy of *Ask for Nothing*, you may order directly from the author. The following prices apply:

Cost per book ....$15.00   _____

Shipping and handling per book ....$4.00   _____

Total Amount ....   _____

To order books, send a check or money order to:

Maxine W. Crane
413 Carriage Drive
Stoneville, NC 27048
mwc1717@embarqmail.com

With all orders, include the following:

Name_____

Address _____

City _____ State_____ Zip _____

Phone Number _____

ORDER FORM

Additional copies of *Without a Father* may be ordered directly from the author. The following prices apply:

Cost per book ....$15.00   _____

Shipping and handling per book ....$4.00   _____

Total Amount ....   _____

To order books, send a check or money order to:

Danny Crane
413 Carriage Drive
Stoneville, NC 27048
mwc1717@embarqmail.com

With all orders, include the following:

Name _____

Address _____

City _____ State _____ Zip _____

Phone Number _____